CAPTIVE SET FREE

CAPTIVE SET FREE

HOW TO FIND FREEDOM THROUGH FORGIVING

VALERIE LIMMER

GREEN SAP PUBLICATIONS

Captive Set Free, copyright © 2022, by Valerie Limmer

All rights reserved. No part of this publication may be reproduced, stored in a retrieval system, or transmitted in any form or by any means, electronic, mechanical, recording or otherwise, without the prior written permission of the author.

All Scripture quotations, unless otherwise indicated, are from the Holy Bible, (NASB®) *New American Standard Bible*®, Copyright © 1960, 1971, 1977 by The Lockman Foundation. Used by permission. All rights reserved. www.lockman.org.

Scripture quotations marked ESV are from the Holy Bible, *English Standard Version*® (ESV®) Copyright © 2001 by Crossway, a publishing ministry of Good News Publishers. All rights reserved. ESV Text Edition: 2016.

Scripture quotations marked KJV are from the Holy Bible, *King James Version*.

Scripture quotations marked NIV are from the Holy Bible, *New International Version*®, NIV® Copyright © 1973, 1978, 1984, 2011 by Biblica, Inc.® Used by permission. All rights reserved worldwide.

Scripture quotations marked NLT are from the Holy Bible, *New Living Translation*, Copyright © 1996, 2004, 2015 by Tyndale House Foundation. Used by permission of Tyndale House Publishers, Inc., Carol Stream, Illinois 60188. All rights reserved.

Scripture quotations marked BLB are from the Holy Bible, *Berean Literal Bible*, Copyright ©2016, 2020 by Bible Hub. Used by Permission. All Rights Reserved Worldwide.

Published by Green Sap Publications
Richmond Hill, Ontario, Canada | www.greensappublications.com
"Every word for Jesus."

Book design copyright © 2022 by Green Sap Publishing. All rights reserved.
Interior design by Green Sap Publishing.
Image: Shutterstock, Inc.
Cover design by Albert Caesar Company, of Raket Creatives.

Printed in the United States of America

ISBN: 978-1-7751879-5-0
1. Religion / Christian Living / Spiritual Growth
2. Religion / Christian Living / Family & Relationships

Appreciation for *Captive Set Free*

Reading Valerie's book moved me to tears. It's so personal and yet also universal, a warm invitation to live a life free of continued pain and bitterness. Well researched and focussed on biblical teachings, she delivers a practical guide to identifying areas that forgiveness can heal. Her understanding of trauma and its impact is a welcome addition to the literature in this area. It's a beautiful book that I will reread to remind myself love with forgiveness is the only way to peace.
—*Sarah Bedley | Children's Counselor, The Yellow Brick House Shelter for Abused Women and Children*

It's safe to say that the need for a deeper understanding of forgiveness is something we all need, and Valerie Limmer tackles the topic in a way that sets the reader at ease, while discussing a richly expressed understanding of forgiveness that is both personal and thoroughly biblical. Valerie writes like the trusted friend you approach over coffee when your heart is heavy, and who encourages with an open Bible and an equally open and vulnerable heart.
—*John Steadman | Director of External Relations, McMaster Divinity College*

Forty years of pastoral ministry have clarified for me that forgiveness may be the greatest gift that we can receive or give, integral to our spiritual and emotional health on our life journey. Valerie describes this precious gift in a biblically sound manner, including her personal reflections and lessons learned. This short book is well worth a read and the chapter reflections merit personal study.
—*Dr. Rodger McCready | Retired Pastor*

Developed through the crucible of Valerie's own experiences, *Captive Set Free* has deeply touched me! It is needed in our world today, a 'must-have' for every Christian's home library.
—*Faith Crosby | Women's Inspirational Speaker*

In *Captive Set Free*, Valerie Limmer unpacks the 'what', 'why' and 'how' of forgiveness in a practical, gentle, yet deeply challenging way. I have already shared some of the insights with colleagues and family as I seek to apply these principles to my life and interactions with others. The case studies, stories and examples from her own life all help to underscore the message that God is not asking the impossible when he calls us to forgive.
—*Treflyn Lloyd-Roberts | General Secretary, International Substance Abuse and Addiction Coalition | CEO, Yeldall Manor Drug & Alcohol Recovery Centre*

Limmer takes a fresh and thorough look at a familiar topic. She is grounded biblically, unflinchingly honest and well researched (from Doidge to Dostoyevsky). With her inclusion of several somatic exercises, this is a powerful and beautiful work. If there is another book as transformational as this one I have never come across it.
—*Cathy Sakiyama | Therapist (PACCP), Certified Professional Counsellor*

Captive Set Free provides a scripture-infused journey that invites readers to unpack the meaning and application of forgiveness. Interspersed with personal accounts of hurt and healing, and filled with practical examples of how to nurture God-honouring relationships, *Captive Set Free* is a must-read for anyone working alongside God's plan for a reconciled world and reconciled relationships through Christ.
—*Joel Gordon | Director of Ministry Partnership and Innovation, The Evangelical Fellowship of Canada*

*For my mother,
who taught me
how to forgive*

Table of Contents

Acknowledgements   *xiii*
Author's Note   *xvii*
Introduction   19

PART I: RELATIONAL DYNAMICS   31
1. Keeping Holy in a Clash   33
2. The Body and the Bride   45
3. Et Tu, Brute?   51
4. Which Fruit?   56
Closing Part I: Food for Thought   *59*

PART II: UNDERSTANDING FORGIVENESS   62
5. What Forgiveness Isn't   64
6. What Forgiveness Is   84
7. How Forgiveness Changed the World   87
8. How Forgiveness Changes the World for Us   96
Closing Part II: Food for Thought   *105*

PART III: OUR FOUNDATION   108
9. Who We Are   110
10. The Importance of Forgiveness   118
11. Forgiveness Belongs to our God   125
12. BC and AD   130
Closing Part III: Food for Thought   *137*

PART IV: FREEDOM IN FORGIVENESS	140
13. How God Forgives Us	142
14. Selling Our Birthright	148
15. Willing Victims?	153
Closing Part IV: Food for Thought	*159*
PART V: HOW TO FORGIVE	162
16. Shaping our Attitudes	163
17. Forgiveness in Practice	174
18. Forgiving Ourselves	196
19. Testing our Forgiveness	201
20. Things That Make Forgiveness Harder	212
Closing Part V: Food for Thought	*217*
PART VI: EXTRAORDINARY FORGIVENESS	220
21. Love Your Enemies	221
22. Standing in the Gap	233
23. Better Than Before	244
Closing Part VI: Food for Thought	*263*
Notes	*267*
Bibliography	*277*
About the Author	*287*

Acknowledgements

THERE ARE SO MANY PEOPLE to thank as this book is published. First, thank you to my husband, Peter, who is always so affirming and encouraging in every step of the writing process. Thank you for your feedback; and for your patience when I need quiet in our little 450-square-foot apartment, or when I have insomnia and need to get up and put the ideas into words to clear my head. You are God's gift to me. Thank you for all that you are, and all that you do.

Second, thank you to my sister, Julia, who recognized the things that made this book special, even when I didn't. Your feedback was beyond valuable in protecting its tone from being edited out of existence. Your encouragement and enthusiasm are so important to me.

Next, thank you to my alpha readers, those people who are experts in their field, and who were the first to comb through my ramblings, gently pointing out those areas that required more thought or refinement. These people are therapists; pastors; people who have suffered types of abuse I haven't; and people from different racial backgrounds than me, who were able to provide important perspectives that, as a white woman, I wouldn't have been able to imagine on my own. Thank you as well to my beta readers, wonderful people who read my manuscript and provided feedback on those parts that were understandable and those places that needed further clarification. My alpha and beta readers included Cathy Sakiyama, Marion Goertz, Miriam Venneri, Rodger McCready, Joel Gordon, Marilyn Nugent, Andrea Lisk, and Melvine Petroff. I'm deeply grateful for your kindness, generosity, and patience.

Lastly, to my editors, Marcia Ford and Lily Yee-Sloan; thank you for your invaluable time, feedback, and encouragement. You have helped to elevate this book beyond my own abilities. Amanda Bauch, thank you for your help in researching those last few elusive references that were inaccessible to me, since I'm hundreds of miles away from an English-language library. I'm so blessed that with you three at my side, the editing process could be one of spiritual fellowship as well as a lot of hard work.

Author's Note

ONE OF THE THINGS I love about God is His creativity. We see it manifested in nature: in the fiery heat of the sun and the frigid cold of space; in the delicacy of a perfectly balanced universe juxtaposed onto forces that, if out of whack, would tear us apart in an instant; in the slow erosion and raging tides that shape and reshape the planet's landscapes; in myriad insects, animals, birds, and fish; and of course, in the playful design of a duck-billed platypus.

God did not make cookie-cutter creations but infused variety even into a single species. He created us as people to be unique, with different fingerprints, skin colours, voices, personalities, facial features—and the list goes on. He knows us intimately, counts every hair on our heads, and inscribes the span of our lives in His Book of Life.

The Bible emphasizes our uniqueness, comparing us to the parts of a body and telling us we have been given different spiritual gifts. Yet, the Bible also says we should work together as members of one body, not rejecting those parts that differ from ourselves. In this way, we add value and depth to each other's existence and experience.

In keeping with our diverse personalities and communication styles, God meets each of us in a way tailored to our spiritual, emotional, and physical makeup. He knows what we will need in order to turn to Him and the preparation required for the struggles and challenges coming our way.

My husband and I are missionaries. During our time in Japan, another missionary and I held weekly Bible studies. We came to an interesting discovery: God not only gives us unique spiritual gifts, but He also seems to choose 'life themes' in the things He teaches us. We might learn a general lesson on some topic and then a few months or years later learn something slightly different and deeper along the same lines. Those lessons often spiral around a theme, and we learn more and more profound lessons. Only our own unwillingness to obey Him limits the depth of these learnings.

Since that Bible study, I've realized that one of my major life themes is forgiveness. I thought it might be helpful to record some of the things I've learnt, as my contribution to the body. The ability to forgive is such a valuable quality—one we can cultivate with God's help and the internal resolve to make it a priority. There is still so much to learn!

Introduction

THE STORIES IN THIS SECTION are adaptations of events that happened to people I've met or who were featured on the news. I've changed their names and some details, but the essentials are true.

THE SHEPHERD AND THE SHOOTER

The room is warm and inviting, a haven from the chilly damp of the evening. One by one, the faithful tromp in. Shaking rain from their umbrellas. Shedding sodden gear. Easing into uncomfortable chairs that are a welcome change from the storm hurling its abuse at those courageous or foolish enough to brave its petulance.

Marcia finishes setup and chooses a seat for herself. This is her favourite day of the week—the day when she and the faithful gather to pray for their church. On many days she's involved in soup kitchens, writing sermons, and counselling parishioners whose problems require the wisdom of Solomon. But Wednesday nights? Those are just for her and the others to meet and be refreshed. She gazes around the circle of chairs and sighs with contentment. Soon they will be full, and soon the power of God will descend on this place.

A few minutes later, Beth, Anna, and Mrs. Potter come in. Everyone—even Marcia—calls her Mrs. Potter. She's so frail.

It's always a thrill to see her enter with cane flailing and jerky steps. How wonderfully God sustains her, even in old age. Behind her is Garth Thompson and—is that a new fellow? A young man in a hooded sweatshirt, slouching, shuffles in.

Praise the Lord! Marcia's heart fills with love. Another young man turning towards Jesus.

She welcomes him and seats him across the circle. That way they can talk easily, but maybe he won't feel intimidated by sitting so close to her.

The room continues to fill, and before long the meeting starts. A brief review of the week's sermon is followed by question-and-answer time. Now, down to business. The prayers are full of passion and courage and trust. All too quickly, an hour passes, then two. Soon it will be time to end. Some parents need to put their children to bed.

The young man has said nothing. He just listens. That's all right with Marcia. *The Word of God will not return to Him empty but will accomplish what He desires.* She remembers the beloved verse. An unfamiliar voice interrupts her thoughts. The young man is speaking.

"—have something for you."

He pulls out a gun.

Oh no.

He fires at the circle.

Mrs. Potter crumples to the ground, then Garth jerks backward. Now it's Marcia's turn.

As she watches the muzzle swing towards her, she doesn't think of ducking. She continues prayer meeting in her mind.

Father, forgive him, for he knows not what he—

The young man flees the scene. The police soon apprehend him.

At the bail hearing, victims' families line the front rows of the courtroom. When the accused is led to his seat, tears begin to flow.

Public outrage is high. How could someone come into a church—the house of God—and desecrate it with such violence? How fitting that the young man was caught so quickly. Now he will face punishment for what he's done, and the losses of all these families will be avenged.

Some relatives indicate they want to address the accused. Now they will give vent to their anger and loss, and begin to heal.

The first woman steps to the microphone. She wrings her Kleenex until it's in tatters, takes a few shaky breaths, and speaks.

"You killed my mother. Helen Potter. She wasn't young, but she was precious to me. My mother was there for me through joy and hardship, births and deaths. You've taken her from me, and that can never be undone. But I want you to know I forgive you."

What?

The public watches in stunned silence as one by one, family members file to the microphone and offer their forgiveness.

The eyes of Christians around the world fill with tears, and our hearts expand with joy at seeing the heart of Jesus revealed in the attitudes and actions of our brothers and sisters in Christ.

Yes! This is what we are all about! This is the love and grace of Jesus, on display for all the world to see.

Three days pass. Less than a week.

A new story breaks in the Christian world.

A famous American evangelist has confessed to having an extramarital affair.

Until now, he has been an example to many of open and honest Christian living. He has never pretended he was holier than anyone else and has freely admitted his mistakes. He's been someone to look up to, someone to emulate.

Now, however, many Christians are angry. This evangelist has not only betrayed his wife. He has betrayed them. The man they've followed has turned out to have deep flaws. How could he do this? How could he choose to lead others when he has committed such a great sin of his own?

Venom and spite overflow on the internet. The same eyes that filled with tears a few days earlier are now narrowed in judgment. The same hearts that expanded in joy are now clenched in hatred.

There was ample forgiveness for the shooter but none for the shepherd.

Remembering

Greta twisted the rings around her fingers. She glanced down, a last check that the blanket on her lap was straight and tidy. Soon the students would file in, and she wanted nothing to distract from her story.

But her glance became a stare. Were those *her* hands resting there? So knobbly—badlands of raised veins and sunken flesh. She had spent so much time living in the past that she often forgot how old she was. Not that she had ever felt young. That had been ripped from her long ago.

The door at the back of the auditorium opened, and the students made an unnaturally hushed entrance. *Their teacher must have told them to be respectful,* Greta thought. Sneakers and backpacks, shuffling along.

The silence was broken before long. A boy made a joke and laughed, voice-cracking adolescence; a girl squealed in indignation; others hissed and restored the hush.

Soon everyone was seated. A caregiver pushed Greta's wheelchair to centre stage, and she began to speak.

"You have been learning about the Holocaust in school. You've been reading textbooks, looking at pictures, memorizing facts. But your teachers want you to also learn about the human side of this horror. They want to put faces on the millions of victims. They want you to see me, to hear my story.

"I was two or three years younger than you are now when I first started hearing of what the Nazis did to Austrian Jews and political dissidents, like my parents."

Greta talked on, voice strong, eyes intense. Together with the students, she journeyed through years of terror and oppression, frantic flight, violent capture, and the camps. Oh, the camps. Cruel guards, incessant hunger, beatings, hopelessness. One sister starving to death, a brother mauled by dogs, a friend subjected to medical 'experiments' with a convulsive end.

"I'm the only one left of my family. The others all died. I don't know why I was left. Why…" Greta's voice trailed off. A few moments later, she continued.

"On the day the Allies freed us from the camp, I physically left that place. But my heart is still there, with my family."

The auditorium was silent.

The teacher stepped to the front, thanked Mrs. Wagner, and turned to the students.

"Mrs. Wagner has agreed to take a few questions. Does anyone have a question?"

The teacher selected five students, who lined up at a microphone. They asked about the usual things—sleeping arrangements in the camp, arrest, life before the camps. The last boy shuffled forward.

"You said your heart is still in the camp. Can you tell me more about your life after? It sounds like you got married and even had kids of your own. Why would your heart still be there?"

She looked at the boy, slouchy clothes and sneakers, backpack slung off the seat behind him, innocence beaming from his face. It was precious, she knew.

And she knew she could never explain to him the terror of knowing it could happen again at any time, whenever human beings devalue each other, whenever they treat cruelty as a matter of course, as part of a job. The overwhelming burden of displaying herself as a living warning to future generations, and yet the crushing necessity of doing so. The panic of violent emotion and flashbacks ever clawing at the edges of conscious thought. The wrongness of life and happiness when all those she'd loved most—

Greta's eyes burned with a fire that age could never dim.

"Those monsters murdered my family. They slaughtered millions upon millions of people. They used natural creativity to create new, imaginative forms of evil. I will never, ever forget what they did. Since then, I've dedicated my life—my life!—to telling of their atrocities. They've taken so much. My family deserves to be remembered, and the Nazis' evil must never be forgotten. I'll never let this go, never."

Greta's breaths came in frenzied gasps. A caregiver stepped forward to administer an oxygen mask and escort her off the stage in her wheelchair.

The students sat in silence for a moment, fierce words echoing in their minds.

...never let this go, never.

Then the whispers started again. The sneakers and backpacks began their shuffle towards the back of the auditorium.

Brothers

The little boy watched his classmates run around the playground. A game of tag. If only he could join in. He turned the stick over in his hand, remembering the difficulty of picking it up in the park earlier. Now he whacked it against his leg braces. It made a lovely tink.

Tink. Tink.

What a great sound.

Tink, tink, tink.

With a sound like that, maybe he could join a band.

Tink.

His special drum. No one else could play.

Tink.

Then the others would know what it was like to be left out.

Tink, tink, tink.

They were always leaving him out, laughing at him.

Tink. Tink.

He only wanted to be part of the group, part of a team. But these stupid leg braces kept getting in the way.

Thwack.

He flung the stick away.

How come he had to be born with broken legs? It wasn't fair. His whole life seemed to be pain. Going from operation to operation, making things a little better but never good enough. Never like the other boys. Never running around and playing tag, like they were doing right now.

He turned around and went away. If he had been a cartoon, a little rain cloud would have appeared over his head as he made his way home.

Home. Mom. Dad. Charlie. At least he had Charlie. That was his brother. He loved Charlie so much. He would do anything for him.

Ah, home now came into view. Almost there. Soon he could rest. Walking took so much work. He was tired.

Charlie was slumped on the front step, looking lonely.

"What is it?" the little boy asked.

"Mom and Dad are fighting again. It's really bad. We shouldn't go in."

A pause.

"How about we go and get some ice cream?" the little boy asked. "I've been saving up my allowance. There should be enough for both of us."

Charlie perked up. He never saved his allowance. He always went straight to the candy shoppe as soon as he got it. That's how they spelt it, with an extra 'pe' at the end. Mom said it made the store seem fancier. Charlie didn't care about fancy. He just knew their candy tasted amazing.

"—just go in and get my money," the little boy was saying.

"Don't let Mom and Dad see you," Charlie said. "They won't be happy if you go in while they're fighting."

"Don't worry, they won't even hear me." The little boy grinned.

He undid his leg braces and crept along the hallway, holding on to the walls, just as he'd practiced ever since his last operation. Totally silent, like a ninja.

"—can't believe you're doing this to me, to the children!" Mom's voice shrieked.

"Stop fighting this. There's nothing you can do to stop me. There's nothing you can do to change my mind."

"What about us? Who'll take care of us when you're gone?" Mom's words changed to sobs.

"Look, I've talked with Jenette, and she's willing to take in one of the kids. I'll take Charlie. You can take the cripple."

The cri—that's me.

The thought felt like a punch to the little boy's chest, and he crumpled to the ground. He couldn't move. He couldn't cry. The world swirled around him.

Was that all he was to Dad? A cripple? Was he like a worthless candy wrapper, easily thrown away? Was he going to lose Charlie—his only friend in the whole world?

He couldn't breathe. He tried to control his gasps and be quiet so Mom and Dad wouldn't hear. He couldn't bear the thought of Dad seeing him on the floor right now.

Luckily, that's when Charlie got worried and came inside.

"Are you okay?" Charlie whispered.

Mom and Dad were lost in their argument. They didn't hear them.

"I fell."

"Hold on, I'll help you."

Working together, the brothers crept out of the house.

Back on the front step, the little boy could hold in his tears no longer. Sobbing, he poured out everything he'd heard. Charlie threw his arms around his brother and cried too.

"They'll never separate us. We won't let them."

And they didn't. Their mother ended up raising them on her own. She cared for them through decades bereft of women's rights, and the boys never lost their bottomless love for her or for each other.

The little boy grew up to be a driven man, outstanding in business and politics. But he never forgot his father's words, and he never forgave the one who had discarded him so cruelly. He became obsessed with insulating himself against future hurt and emotionally isolated himself from all meaningful relationships, even with his wife and children. Deep down, he ever remained the little boy on the porch, sobbing out shards of his heart, with Charlie's arms around him.

Part I
Relational Dynamics

FORGIVENESS. THAT WORD HAS the power to conjure up an immediate visceral response in us. Our reactions may vary, depending on our state of mind and recent events in our lives.

- When we're at fault, forgiveness seems like an oasis in a desert of wrongdoing. It's a promise of hope in a landscape of regret.

- When we've been newly wronged, forgiveness can feel threatening. We would rather ignore it and indulge in self-pity or indignation. But it looms, wagging its finger and demanding action.

- When some time has passed, the idea shifts and weighs heavier on us. We know we ought to forgive and can no longer put it off. We sigh deeply and begin trudging along the winding path whose destination beckons at a weary end.

Perhaps your mental pictures and emotions differ from mine when you hear the word 'forgiveness', but I suspect one thing is the same for all of us—when we receive it, forgiveness is a relief; when we have to give it, forgiveness can be arduous. In fact, forgiving is one of the most difficult things on earth to do.

1
Keeping Holy in a Clash

Disunity is one of Satan's greatest strategies against the church.
AJITH FERNANDO, TEACHING DIRECTOR OF
YOUTH FOR CHRIST

CONFLICT IS INEVITABLE IN THE human experience, and is it any wonder? I'm a Canadian from multicultural Toronto. As a nation, we Canadians pride ourselves on our skill in interacting with people of many nationalities and our welcoming attitude towards people from various backgrounds.

We all come from different personal cultures, whether or not we're from a foreign country. Sometimes we fool ourselves into thinking that if we're from the same nation and society as someone else, we must have a solid basis for understanding. However, the country and town where we grew up are only two factors in determining our personal culture. Different cultures may stem from contrasting vocabularies and internal dictionaries that influence the things we say and hear, individual motivations and ambitions, family dynamics in childhood, and distinct emotional backgrounds.

My husband, Peter, and I are examples of divergent cultures. We both came from middle-class families and grew up in neighbouring towns. All four of our parents are Christians.

But the cultures we brought into our marriage were poles apart. His heritage is from Japan and England. Mine is dominantly Eastern European. His family is quiet; mine is loud. His understands personal space and belongings; mine has no such comprehension. His family values music and problem-solving; mine tends to be linguistic and mathematical. His is mostly in Christian ministry or government service; mine is filled with professionals. These differences led to some unexpected friction early in our marriage as we learned to navigate our new relationship and the expectations we both carried.

Personal variations affect our workplaces and friendships as well. Though you and I may be emotionally healthy, not everyone we befriend may be so. Perhaps someone has recently been hurt. They may be sensitive or combative when their emotional bruises are touched. Some people may be healthy in one area and dysfunctional in another.

Therapist and reconciliation consultant Marion Goertz is fond of saying anger acts as the protective 'big brother' to the more fundamental emotions of sadness, fear, abandonment, and betrayal.[1] Conflict may stem from unmet needs or people protecting themselves from being vulnerable. The old standbys—hunger, fatigue, and stress—are ingredients of irritability. Those dieting or trying to quit smoking, both of which include hunger *and* stress, may tend to be testier.

Considering all these differences, coupled with our sometimes-mistaken assumption that we understand those around us, is it any wonder tumult is inevitable? Given the complexity of a single relationship, it's no surprise that there is conflict. It surprising there's not *more* of it.

Many worldly relationships drift towards discord, aggression, and gossip. Sadly, Christian relationships often drift in the same direction.

A Japanese person once told me that in his culture, actions matter more than words. By always watching those around them, the Japanese learn who people are. They say those who demonstrate consistency between their words and actions have 'true hearts' or hearts of sincerity.

Our friends, families, neighbours, and colleagues who aren't Christians are often just as observant. While I was working as an engineer in Canada, one of my co-workers called me out on having said "Oh, God!" in a conversation. He knew Christians tend to shy away from that phrase because using God's name so casually dishonours the One we love. I was surprised at such scrutiny.

Fortunately, that wording is not in my active vocabulary, so there was no chance it had crossed my lips. I could assure him I had said, "Oh, gosh!"—though the "sh" turned out to be quieter than I'd intended. (*I'll have to watch that*, I thought.)

Japanese people and those who aren't Christians seem to have hit upon an important truth that Western Christians sometimes overlook. In a sinful world, consistency between our words and deeds is of paramount importance. If we say we believe something but our actions don't bear this out, perhaps we should re-examine our beliefs.

The Bible tells us the best way to measure a person's convictions is to examine his or her behaviour. If we accept this as axiomatic, what we find may startle us. George Barna, founder of The Barna Group, has carried out hundreds of sociological studies on the interplay of faith, culture, and behaviour in the United States. According to one survey, there's statistically no difference between Western Christians and non-Christians[2] in divorce rates, level of community involvement, the incidence of filing lawsuits, and donating to (or volunteering at) non-profit organizations. Though Christians seem to encourage people more and watch violent or sexually explicit movies less, those who are not Christians give more to the poor and homeless.[3]

According to Barna, for most behaviours, there is no statistically significant difference between Christians and the rest of the world. Those who claim to follow Christ try to maintain the purity of their minds a little more but care less for the poor in practical ways. Does this remind you of anyone in the Bible?

During His life on earth, Jesus said, "Beware of the scribes who like to walk around in long robes, and like respectful greetings in the marketplaces, and chief seats in the synagogues and places of honor at banquets, who devour widows' houses, and for appearance's sake offer long prayers; these will receive greater condemnation" (Mark 12:38–40).

The scribes liked to pretend they were pure and holy, but their actions towards the poor revealed the true state of their hearts. If we care only about our perceived purity and not our actual behaviour, we're acting like the scribes. Were we living in the time of Jesus, He would condemn us too.

This begs the question: if the conduct of Christians does not differ from that of the world in so many measurable areas, how will we act when it comes to forgiveness?

Our Western culture prizes individualism and truth. On the other hand, Eastern cultures value unity with one's groups—even at the expense of truth. Saying something false doesn't even fall onto the truth/lie continuum unless it causes someone harm. Instead, each person's dignity is the highest aim, and individuals are expected to work together with the group for the greater good.

In Japan, large black, red, and orange centipedes, called *mukade*, are plentiful. Some people think of the centipede as a symbol for Japanese society. A leg—a part of the communal entity, though not self-sufficient—symbolizes each person working together with the other legs to draw the insect towards its destination. Conversations in Japanese tend to be much longer than in English because participants work relationship-building into every point of contact. No deadline, no matter how urgent, is more important than the web of relationships embedded in each person's life.

In the West, we sometimes misidentify what unity is. The absence of conflict is not unity, just as the absence of disease is not health. Sometimes the most unified bonds are ones that face strife but also work towards loving resolution. We can have a sense of confidence that may not be present in relationships that have never faced these things. Such confidence is born from an acknowledgement that we don't have to avoid conflict or agree on everything. There can be disagreements—sometimes even unpleasant ones—but at the bedrock, there will always be respect and love.

When we flee conflict, we rob ourselves of the ability to experience true unity, healing, and confidence in our spiritual relationships. We also rob God of the chance to demonstrate His power and exhibit His love, forgiveness, and grace both through and to us. As church planter Aaron Loy once wrote, "Some of God's best work happens in the mess."

In my time as a missionary in Japan, I've been learning a lot about what it means to live in harmony. The preservation of the *wa*, a sense of social unity, is crucial in the Japanese culture. By comparison, our native North American culture seems increasingly harsh, impatient, and rigid to us. I sometimes wonder if we lose something priceless when we discard the importance of harmony in favour of other, often-opposite goals.

As with so many things, the general attitudes of society have made their way into North American churches. The Bible often mentions unity as a goal within the body of Christ. In North America, we treat it as a byproduct but not an objective. We quote verses like "How good and how pleasant it is for brothers to dwell together in unity!" (Psalm 133:1) while ignoring the implications of Scriptures that urge us to "attain to the unity of the faith" (Ephesians 4:13).

Attaining to the unity of the faith. This sounds like a goal to me. The apostle Paul talks about the need to be "diligent to preserve the unity of the Spirit" (Ephesians 4:3). Unity doesn't just happen. We're told to diligently seek and guard it. We have fallen far short of this lofty aim in North America.

Peter and I had each been Christians for more than thirty years when we realized we had missed some profound lessons in the apostle Paul's teachings.

> I urge Euodia and I urge Syntyche to live in harmony in the Lord. Indeed, true companion, I ask you also to help these women who have shared my struggle in the cause of the gospel, together with Clement also and the rest of my fellow workers, whose names are in the book of life.
>
> Rejoice in the Lord always; again I will say, rejoice! Let your gentle spirit be known to all men. The Lord is near. Be anxious for nothing, but in everything by prayer and supplication with thanksgiving let your requests be made

known to God. And the peace of God, which surpasses all comprehension, will guard your hearts and your minds in Christ Jesus.

Finally, brethren, whatever is true, whatever is honorable, whatever is right, whatever is pure, whatever is lovely, whatever is of good repute, if there is any excellence and if anything worthy of praise, dwell on these things. The things you have learned and received and heard and seen in me, practice these things, and the God of peace will be with you.

Philippians 4:2–9

At the start of the passage above, my Bible has a subheading that reads "Think of Excellence". The subheading in Peter's Bible reads: "Exhortation, Encouragement, and Prayer". These topical headings were added later by editors, *not* by translators. I don't know if such additions blinded us to understanding this passage, but they can't have helped.

These headings, and every sermon we had ever heard on this text, made it seem as though Paul was discussing several subjects. Yet perhaps this passage was not so disjointed after all. Perhaps it was all about the same thing. Instead of giving a brief spiel to two women in conflict followed by general exhortations to the church, perhaps Paul was still talking about conflict after the first paragraph. Could it be that this entire section was a list of instructions on the mentality

Euodia and Syntyche should adopt to avoid sinning in the midst of their clash?

I now believe Philippians 4:2–9 is a primer on how to live holy lives even in the presence of conflict. Following these guidelines, we can make forgiveness, restoration, and unity simpler for ourselves. Let's take a closer look.

1. Rejoice.

"Rejoice in the Lord always; again I will say, rejoice!" (Philippians 4:4)

Joy is one of the first things that leaves us when we are in a conflict. According to Paul, rejoicing is also one of the first things we should administer as an antidote, because it denotes a trust in God and a recognition that we don't have to tense up and solve our problems by ourselves. God knows what's going on, and He knows what will come next. We can rejoice in His love and care for us, and be confident in our future because He has it in His hands.

2. Don't retaliate.

"Let your gentle spirit be known to all men." (4:5)

The Greek term for 'gentle spirit' often refers to displaying a gentle or kind spirit when retaliation would be normal.[4] Our unexpected tenderness should be so consistent that we become known for it.

3. Don't blow things out of proportion.
"The Lord is near." (4:5)

The original Greek meaning of "near" is unclear. It may refer to near in place or near in time.[5] We may interpret "the Lord is near" in two different ways:

- The Lord is physically nearby. He sees what is happening to you, and He sees what you are doing. Be assured He will not ignore any injustice you encounter nor any sins you may commit in this conflict.

- The Lord is nearby temporally. He is coming soon, so don't blow this current conflict out of proportion. It's small potatoes in light of eternity.

4. Pray, give thanks, and allow God's peace to fill your heart.
"Be anxious for nothing, but in everything by prayer and supplication with thanksgiving let your requests be made known to God. And the peace of God, which surpasses all comprehension, will guard your hearts and your minds in Christ Jesus." (4:5–6)

If rejoicing is one of the first things to leave at the start of conflict, then anxiety is one of the first things to arrive. Here, Paul encourages us to lay our anxieties at Jesus' feet and replace them with an attitude of thanksgiving.

Giving thanks can change our perspectives like almost nothing else. When we discover things to thank God for, our fundamental experience is changed. Just as with rejoicing, the act of giving thanks expresses trust in our heavenly Father. It enables God's peace to flow in, replaces anxiety, and guards our hearts and minds. How closely my heart and mind need to be guarded, especially in conflict!

5. Guard your heart and concentrate on the good.

"Finally, brethren, whatever is true, whatever is honorable, whatever is right, whatever is pure, whatever is lovely, whatever is of good repute, if there is any excellence and if anything worthy of praise, dwell on these things." (4:8)

There are two possible interpretations for this point. Both have their merits and could be true at the same time.

- When we're in conflict, our minds tend to spool, rehashing each thing the other person has said and done. We become obsessed with their misdeeds, whether real or fantasized. If we let this happen, we multiply our chances of sinning and allowing bitterness to enter the equation. It is possible, however, to take our thoughts captive.[6] We can choose not to engage in venomous obsessions but to fix our eyes on Jesus—and therefore on things that are honourable, right, pure, lovely, and so on.

- Jesus' command to love each other as He loved us doesn't stop when conflict begins. We are under obligation to value one another at all times. We can do this by wilfully focusing our attention on the good and lovely things still true of the other person. In this way, we retain a sense of love for them and are able to bless those who curse us, do good to those who hate us, and pray for those who mistreat us.

Do you find such thoughts as challenging as I do? None of us can make these changes without Jesus' help. How wonderful that He has promised to never leave nor forsake us and to complete the good work He has started in us!

2

The Body and the Bride

The human body has many parts, but the many parts make up one whole body. So it is with the body of Christ.

1 CORINTHIANS 12:12, NLT

WE OFTEN USE THE WORD 'church' to refer to a place where people of similar beliefs meet. When I was growing up, pastors worked hard to educate congregants that this term had a second meaning: "The church is not this building. It's the people—you and your fellow Christians."

These days, such an explanation is often unnecessary, yet Satan has a sneaky way of distorting the truth using minimal modifications. Changing only one letter or word of a true sentence makes a lie much more difficult to discern.

Here is the truth:
We are the church.

Here is the lie:
I am the church.

These days, people may say, "I am the church. I don't need to go to meetings."
This is not true.

We—together—are the church. Singly, we are Christ-followers. But when we stop obeying His commands, we no longer follow Christ. God's Word instructs us to continually gather together. As seminary professor Brenda Colijn puts it, "Salvation is not a private individual experience without social consequences: we are born into a family."

No family is perfect. We all encounter hurts, some profound and far-reaching, at the hands of people we love. However, God has given us to each other for a reason. Families often stand by one another in situations when everyone else bails out.

Yes, our families may disappoint and discourage us. Yes, they may be manipulative. Yes, they may be broken. But so are we.

We cannot unhook ourselves from our fellow believers. We are connected to them. God uses two metaphors to illustrate this reality.

The Body of Christ

The Bible likens Christians to the body of Christ. Each person represents a different body part, and each part belongs to all the others. Christ has knitted us together. The blood He shed on the cross runs through the veins of His body, bringing nourishment and rejuvenation to everyone.

When you or I hurt, Jesus hurts too. That's what it means to be part of the same body. When one member feels pain, so do the others. When we cause Jesus' people to suffer, we also cause Him to suffer. Abuse and mistreatment within the body become self-mutilation.

If the Christian church is to function as a body, bound together for survival, then the thought of severing our connection to it deserves the same gravity as considering whether to sever one of our own limbs. Amputation may be necessary to prevent the gangrene of spiritual abuse from spreading. But it is not a decision to be taken lightly. We cannot afford to be reactionary. If a fingernail scratches our arm, we would never think of taking a chainsaw to the finger.

When we remove ourselves from Christ's church, we engage in spiritual amputation—not from our own body but from Jesus'.

Consider what may happen to a limb continuously severed and reattached to different parts of a body. We need only observe someone who has undergone multiple nose jobs for a clue. One day, the nose collapses and cannot be rebuilt. Following numerous amputations, a limb can no longer be repaired or successfully reattached. It dies.

If I make a habit of uprooting myself from existing relationships, sooner or later I'll be unable to form attachments at all. My ability to sustain healthy bonds dies.

Our hearts cry, "There must be a better way!" And they're right. But Satan, that wily devil, skilfully mixes the truth with a lie. He takes the primal groaning of all creation at a world that is unjust and incomplete and twists it to suit his own purposes.

- "If I go to another church, I'll find people who are godlier, who won't hurt me like this. It will be better."
- "I don't need to go to church. Being a Christian is about a relationship between Jesus and me. The time of the church is over. The better way is to build my bond with Jesus—just the two of us."

Can you hear Satan's crafty hiss?

The truth is that we were indeed made for a better way. We were made for freedom and joy. But the solution does not lie outside ourselves, in a different church or group of believers. The answer lies within our very own hearts. And now, we are charged to find it.

The Bride of Christ

The Bible also uses the metaphor of a bride and groom when speaking of Christ and His church. Those of us who are protective by nature, whether of spouses, kids, or other family and friends, will understand the trauma of witnessing the ones we love being shamed or abused. Just as a loving husband is protective of his wife, so Jesus is protective of His bride.

When hurt by people in the church, we may crave retribution and want the whole world to know about the injustice we've suffered. We want to shame others as they've shamed us, to showcase our own righteousness against the backdrop of their unrighteousness. We think this will achieve justice. After all, doesn't the Bible permit taking an "eye for an eye" (Exodus 21:24)?

And yet, during His life on earth, Jesus elevated the standard we are to live by (see Matthew 5:38–42). He said, "Whatever you do to the least of these, you do to Me" (Matthew 25:40, my paraphrase). This means when we dishonour our fellow Christians, we dishonour Christ Himself. When we put our outrage on display for all the world to see, how agonizing it must be for Jesus to see His bride endure public disgrace!

When wounded, we are more susceptible to the lies of Satan. He blinds us to truth in favour of a distorted reality that he's happy to provide. Hurt people tend to hurt other people. If we publicly humiliate the bride of Christ, the offenders are not the ones who are most disgraced. We destroy the reputation of Christ and glory in our own shame—one born of hypocrisy. We are happy to accept Jesus' forgiveness but are unwilling to extend it to others. Our degradation is not caused by those who have mistreated us, but by our own deeds and heart attitudes.

The apostle Paul wrote:

> To this end also we pray for you always, that our God will count you worthy of your calling, and fulfill every desire

for goodness and the work of faith with power, *so that the name of our Lord Jesus will be glorified in you*, and you in Him, according to the grace of our God and the Lord Jesus Christ.

2 Thessalonians 1:11–12, emphasis mine

These verses are remarkable because they hint at a staggering decision Jesus has made. He has chosen to be glorified *in* us, not *apart* from us.

"When a guy marries an amazing woman," my husband, Peter, once pointed out, "people look at him and think he must be extraordinary to have snagged such a woman. They think more highly of him because of the woman he's married."

Marriage is a metaphor for our relationship with Christ. In the idealized union of the Bible, the bride (the church) brings honour to her husband (Christ). She is His crown. If we devalue Christ's church, we diminish His glory.

To put it another way, when we bash the bride, we dishonour the groom.

3

Et Tu, Brute?

"It is not an enemy who taunts me—
I could bear that.
Instead, it is you—my equal,
my companion and close friend.
What good fellowship we once enjoyed
as we walked together to the house of God."

PSALM 55:12–14

BEING HURT BY PEOPLE IN the family of God feels especially egregious. They should know better, shouldn't they? Aren't Christians supposed to act like Christ? Shouldn't they love others more than themselves? Shouldn't they be gentle and kind?

These questions may swirl around in our heads. It's difficult to cut through the confusion to get at the essential issue: why are Christians so hurt by other Christians?

1. OUR EXPECTATIONS

The relational dynamic in churches differs from elsewhere. We open ourselves to fellow believers more quickly than to other acquaintances because we engage in mutually meaningful interactions, like worshipping God and sharing prayer requests.

When we're transparent, we're also more vulnerable. This is as it should be, because the body of Christ was created so members would spur one another on in love. We need to be spiritually and relationally receptive for this to happen.

Every good thing has the potential to be used malevolently. Deeper relationships lead to a greater capacity for distress. When this happens, we can be caught off guard. We don't expect Christians to hurt us. Surprise somehow makes the pain worse.

Does this mean wounded Christians are too sensitive? Or are the Christian perpetrators too callous to the feelings of others?

Our expectations play a vital role in our experience. We may think Christians should be more 'perfected' than the rest of the world. But sometimes these changes may not be visible.

God's work often prioritizes different areas than you or I would focus on, were we given divine authority. The perfecting process is achingly slow. It may take years to submit to God's will in just one tiny area. Perceptible results may take decades to appear.

Does this mean interacting with other Christians is dangerous and foolhardy? Are people who have been hurt and have sworn off church actually onto something? After all, they've decided to forgo vulnerability and spare themselves more pain.

Such a mentality does not follow biblical standards. Pain—and the avoidance of it—is not to be our chief concern. Remember, the Bible says, "And let us consider how to stimulate one another to love and good deeds, *not forsaking our own assembling together*, as is the habit of some, but encouraging one another; and all the more as you see the day drawing near" (Hebrews 10:24–25, emphasis mine).

This leaves us with a choice: do we close down and protect ourselves from all potential harm—and all potential good—or do we take the courageous step that opens us to the possibility of pain? Do we refuse to give in and instead remain open to encountering the good, as well as the hurt, in our future?

Jesus never said our lives will be devoid of pain. In fact, He foretold the opposite: tribulation, the inevitability of hardship and suffering.

Somewhere along the way, many Western Christians have allowed the prosperity gospel—which says those who have faith will be blessed with extravagant wealth and success—to infiltrate our thinking. This version doesn't assume physical riches. It comes in a different form: we don't expect to suffer. Living in the West, we've gotten soft. We expect life to be easy.

When sick, we assume God will heal us according to our faith. Sometimes He does. But those whom God chooses not to heal don't deserve to have their faith maligned. Healing may not be in God's plans for some people before they get to heaven.

Though the able-bodied may be kind and sympathetic, a person can only understand certain aspects of a life with disability if he or she has also experienced debilitation for a significant length of time. If all Christians were healthy, who would spiritually minister to the sick and disabled on this immersive level? Some of the most meaningful ministries flow from the depth of experience.

In the same way, if we never endure interpersonal conflict, what spiritual advice and comfort will we have to offer those who are themselves embroiled in conflict?

Hurt often stems from mismatched expectations and reality. This doesn't mean you and I should approach relationships with fatalistic skepticism. It *does* mean we should develop ties, to our churches and other Christians, that are strong enough to weather the eventual storms of conflict and pain.

2. SPIRITUAL WARFARE

When we encounter hurt, we tend to attribute its cause to people we can see. Too often, we ignore the spiritual element. Satan sometimes targets Christians with his unholy schemes *more* than he targets people who aren't Christians. If the enemy can create a horrific enough situation, he can incapacitate Christ's followers and do a lot to discredit Christ's work in the eyes of people who don't follow Him.

When we handle hurt improperly, we can be distracted and crippled from receiving the good things God has for us. This can impair our relationships with fellow believers and destroy our witness to those who don't yet know Christ.

As Christians, we need to be aware that "our struggle is not against flesh and blood, but against the rulers, against the powers, against the world forces of this darkness, against the spiritual forces of wickedness in the heavenly places" (Ephesians 6:12). Satan fights dirty. He "prowls around like a roaring lion, seeking someone to devour" (1 Peter 5:8) and "masquerades as an angel of light" (2 Corinthians 11:14, niv). He will use every trick in the book—and many that no human has thought of!—to undermine Jesus and His work on earth. We cannot afford to ignore his influence.

Satan may be more powerful than us, but he is *not* more powerful than Jesus. Thank God our Saviour is far greater than Satan will ever be! You and I have nothing to fear from our enemy as long as we stay close to Jesus, but we do need to be aware of Satan's strategies and influence.

4
Which Fruit?

Whoever opts for revenge should dig two graves.
CONFUCIUS

WHEN YOU AND I CHOOSE not to forgive, we bury the better part of ourselves—the part that has the potential to follow and honour Jesus. Our hearts get sick. They begin to show symptoms of poor health, much as the body does during illness.

Imagine this scenario.

You've been wounded by someone. We'll call this person 'Jude'. Then you encounter a third party. We'll call her 'Jane'. She also knows Jude but has no idea what he's done. When Jane speaks well of Jude, what's your first reaction?

My thoughts usually go something like this:

Good, Jude hasn't hurt Jane too.

Gee, Jane sure is praising Jude a lot. She wouldn't be saying such complimentary things if she knew what he had done to me.

I wish she knew. Then she would see how much I've suffered. She would think well of me instead of Jude.

We begin to interpret anything good said about our 'Judes' as insults or threats against our own personhood and value as people.

Other times, we may try to rationalize our desire to gossip under the guise of concern. For example: *Jane is so sweet. She's developing a closer relationship with Jude. I'm concerned for her. He's such a twisted person, and she's so innocent. I should warn her of what he's capable of before she gets hurt!*

We experience dark pleasure when we open our mouths to tell our painful stories. Our spiritual symptoms spiral from gossip and jealousy to bitterness and hatred. Eventually, they work their way into physical reality. Doctors say bitterness can manifest in insomnia, heightened blood pressure, increased back pain and headaches,[1] altered metabolism and immune response, decreased organ function, and even emerging new diseases.[2]

At its crux, the choice not to forgive is a choice to embrace resentment. This is the only alternative, and it yields its own fruit. Most of us are familiar with the fruit of the Spirit:

> Love, joy, peace, patience, kindness, goodness, faithfulness, gentleness, self-control; against such things there is no law.
> GALATIANS 5:22–23

However, immediately before this, Paul lists "the deeds of the flesh", which are natural consequences of resentment. They include:

> enmities, strife, jealousy, outbursts of anger, disputes, dissensions, factions, envying.
> GALATIANS 5:20–21

The Bible labels bitterness as a root because it grows like a plant. When we water and nurture it, bitterness affects our other relationships. Hebrews tells us that in the end it causes trouble and defiles many—not just ourselves.

The effects of bitterness are opposite to those of the Spirit:

Fruit of the Spirit	Fruit of Bitterness
Love	Hatred
Joy	Envy
Peace	Inward: jealousy; outward: strife
Patience	Outbursts of anger
Kindness	Enmity
Goodness	All the traits of bitterness
Gentleness	Hostility
Faithfulness	Factions
Self-control	Outbursts of anger

Paul ends his list of fleshly fruit saying, "Those who practice such things will not inherit the kingdom of God" (Galatians 5:21). The stakes are high both now and in eternity—actually, they couldn't be higher.

Closing Part I

Food for Thought

IF WE LOOK CLOSELY, we can see the wisdom of men at odds with the wisdom of God in many circumstances.

What does the world say about broken relationships? Author David Augsburger sums it up: "Rejecting all relationships that have failed us is the most common 'solution' in our contemporary Western culture, among Christians and non-Christians alike. Cut off the old connections, withdraw from all interactions, live at a distance, avoid intimacy or involvement. Above all, do not risk working at forgiveness."[1]

It's true: forgiveness is a risk. To some it may seem foolhardy. What greater folly is there than opening oneself up—during hostility, no less!—to someone who has already caused hurt? What if he's unwilling to see the error of his ways? What if she compounds her wrongdoing?

When we've experienced conflict, abuse, or other hurts, we can become prisoners of the things that have been done to us. Forgiveness enables us to step out of our own imprisonment, approach both God and our adversaries with clean hearts, and enter into the glorious abundance Jesus has prepared for us.

The Bible says the wisdom of God appears to the world as foolishness. Humanly speaking, the risks are high. Yet this does not take God and His ways into account. He, after all, forgave us when we were still His enemies. Will we choose to trust Him? Will we choose to emulate Him and forgive, just as Jesus forgave us?

Going Deeper

1. Why is forgiving someone so hard?

2. In this section, we discussed how we can apply Philippians 4:2–8 to resolving conflict. Which of Paul's five points is easiest for you? Which is most challenging?

3. The Bible says Jesus is glorified *in* us, not *apart* from us. How does this change the way you view Christ's church? What does this mean for you?—i.e., what responsibility do you have?

4. Why is it important not to give up meeting with fellow Christians, even when we have been hurt? In your answer, talk about the example God sets for us in this and the opportunities for growth we may miss if we stop meeting regularly with other Christians.

Part II

Understanding Forgiveness

LET'S NOW CONSIDER WHAT FORGIVENESS is and isn't. At first, you may think this is a rudimentary exercise, not worth our time and bother, but I would suggest there is much we don't understand about forgiveness.

The popular Harry Potter books, written by J.K. Rowling, follow a boy wizard through his adolescence into adulthood. He attends a school of magic where he meets a cruel teacher named Severus Snape. Eventually, he discovers Snape is far more complex than he realized. Snape has made immense sacrifices for his welfare. At the end of the series, Harry names his son 'Severus' in recognition of his teacher's hidden character.

One day I discovered an article in which J.K. Rowling explained to fans why Harry Potter named his son after Severus Snape. She said it was because of forgiveness and gratitude.[1] The connection seemed obvious to some people but was lost on others. This piece wasn't just printed in an obscure magazine. It made all the major entertainment publications. With that, I realized forgiveness had become a foreign concept in our culture. It's important we understand it before moving on.

To start, take some time to consider what your definition of forgiveness may be. Jot down some notes; they don't have to be eloquent or even organized. Sometimes complicated vocabulary can mask deficiencies in our thought processes and explanations. So, use simple language. Imagine talking to an adult from another country, who can understand complex concepts but not long words.

After you've finished this exercise, ask yourself the following questions:

- Are there any gaps in my thinking?
- Is anything unclear?

The struggle to define a concept can help us achieve new insights. Don't be afraid to close this book, grab a hot beverage, pen, and paper, and mull it over. This definition is important—perhaps one of the most important you will ever consider. So, let's invest some time and effort in it.

5
What Forgiveness Isn't

It is better to understand little than to misunderstand a lot.
ANATOLE FRANCE, NOBEL PRIZE-WINNING WRITER

I ONCE KNEW A CHRISTIAN man who left a trail of broken relationships wherever he went. If an employee moved on from his company, he was offended.

There's no acceptable reason to leave, he seemed to think.

When people disagreed with him, he took it personally. He never resolved conflicts. He became so used to breaking off contact that he began to sever relationships with people who were inconvenient to him, even when there had been no conflict.

One day, I talked with him about how to deal with relational pain.

"Forgiveness means we are no longer bound to the people who have hurt us," he said. "We are freed from our previous hurts, and we can just walk away."

Hearing his words and seeing his life, I couldn't help feeling sad. He seemed to think he had forgiven the people he'd cut off. If you'd asked those people, though, I'm pretty sure *they* wouldn't have thought he'd forgiven them!

Fallacy #1: Forgiveness is a feeling.

How many times have you heard the phrase 'follow your heart'? A common theme in all the best romances, it usually glides off the lips of the main character's trusted friend just at the point when all seems lost and only a great, daring leap into the unknown will save the day. People who follow their hearts are portrayed as courageous, willing to put themselves on the line for the dream of love. We are encouraged to follow our heart and are admired for it.

But the Bible warns us about a sinister side to this paradigm: "The heart is deceitful above all things, and desperately wicked" (Jeremiah 17:9, KJV). If our hearts are so wicked, then following them could be harmful.

We're left with two conflicting points of view—one looking upon the heart as something good, courageous, and passionate, the other viewing it as something decayed, destructive, and deceitful.

We all want to think the best of ourselves. That's one reason the idea of a brave and beautiful heart is so attractive. When we consider other people, though, we find it easier to believe bad things of them. Do we naturally attribute beauty and courage to the person who cuts us off in traffic? What about the mugger? The politician?

In comparing the ways we view ourselves and others, we see a strange dichotomy at work—that our souls are mainly beautiful but others' are often ugly. We gravitate towards giving ourselves the benefit of the doubt while being stingy with other people in similar circumstances. As writer and public speaker Stephen M.R. Covey put it, "We tend to judge ourselves by our intentions and others by their behavior."

Let's do a thought experiment. What if I inadvertently cut someone off in traffic? To the person now behind me, I may appear selfish. From my perspective, I'm in a hurry and taking advantage of a small opening between cars. Is my spirit somehow beautiful and ugly at the same time?

God created us in His image, so an element of beauty—just as God is beautiful—exists in the heart of every person. That said, we've all been saddled with the decay and destruction of our sinful natures. Our hearts' beauty has been corrupted by the cancer of sin. It's always terminal.

The Bible refers to the 'heart' as the seat of our feelings. Psychologists tell us emotions can be transient, unreliable, and unpredictable.[1] So, we probably shouldn't allow them to be the only guide for our actions because they can be misleading.

Feelings aren't inherently sinful, just as temptation isn't sin. Jesus was tempted, but the Bible tells us He was without sin. The *actions* we take are what may be wrong. I once heard a pastor say, "You can't stop a bird from flying over your head and pooping on it, but you can stop it from nesting in your hair." His point was that we can't prevent random temptations or feelings from coming our way. However, we can choose whether to actively engage them.

God created us as beings like Himself—ones who at different points encounter the full spectrum of emotion. Anger, for instance, is not a sin. God feels anger particularly when He sees those He loves being mistreated. For example, Jesus became angry when He saw the religious leaders of His day excluding vulnerable foreigners from worshipping at the temple.[2]

It's what we do with the emotion that can be sinful. If we choose to dwell on angry feelings without forgiveness, they can turn into bitterness—which is sin. We may decide to put bitterness into action, perhaps seeking revenge for wrongs suffered. This, too, is sinful.

How many times have we heard the phrase 'the heart wants what the heart wants'? This line is often used as people helplessly follow wherever their emotions lead them. But we have more control over our thoughts and feelings than we think.

Let's remember the fallacy—forgiveness is a feeling—for a moment. The world would have us believe that forgiveness, like thankfulness, is a feeling. However, forgiveness is actually about 80 percent decision and 20 percent feeling. The idea that we're incapable of controlling our thoughts and emotions is a lie. We can decide to forgive, even if we don't feel like doing so. Our choices can transcend our emotions.

"But wait a minute," someone may say, "if I try to forgive without first *feeling* forgiving, am I not being hypocritical? If I'm not acting according to my feelings, am I not living a lie?"

A few assumptions underpin this question. As Christians, when we're considering a topic, it's always best to go back to the Scriptures as the basis for our reasoning. They are the most reliable source of truth and as the Word of God are not subject to the same errors that can creep into our human thinking.[3]

Some people say that if a person's words, feelings, and actions do not match up, he or she is a hypocrite. Is there a flaw in this? Let's consider Jesus as our role model. Was He a hypocrite?

Most of us would agree Jesus was God's antithesis to the Pharisees' worldview. He consistently challenged their attitudes and actions, labelling them "hypocrites", a "brood of vipers", and "whitewashed tombs" (Matthew 12:34, 23:13, 23:27). He despised hypocrisy and exhorted His followers to match their deeds to their words. In fact, Jesus modelled this for us. He didn't just teach that we should love our enemies; He loved His enemies. He didn't just teach that we should forgive; He forgave.

Now comes a tricky question. When He was being tortured on the cross, did Jesus *feel* like forgiving the people killing Him?

As God, perhaps He did. But surely His human side didn't feel like doing this and was tempted not to do so. Yet He prayed, "Father, forgive them, for they know not what they do" (Luke 23:34, ESV).

We are left with two options: either Jesus was a hypocrite, or our definition is wrong.

While in university, I was involved with a Christian student group that emphasized evangelism. We regularly distributed fliers that challenged people in their relationships with God. Some were about how to have a relationship with Him in the first place. One was on how to live a life filled and empowered by the Holy Spirit.

That booklet illustrated the connection between fact, faith, and feelings using the analogy of a train.

"You put faith (fuel) in the facts (engine), and the feelings (train cars) will follow," it read.[4] If we place our feelings in the right position, then fact and faith pull them along. Faith is opposed not to reason but to sight. Though faith is not limited to reason, the two can work together.[5] We can exert control over our emotions, even though they are fickle.[6]

So, where does this leave our definition of the word 'hypocrite'?

- What if hypocrisy is less about our feelings than about our words and behaviour?

- What if it matters only whether our words and deeds match?

- What if it's okay if our feelings do not immediately line up with our actions and decisions?

A hypocrite, by the dictionary's definition, is someone whose deeds and words don't align.[7] If I give a speech on the destructiveness of fossil fuels, exhort people to buy more energy-efficient cars, and purchase a gas-guzzling SUV for myself, then I am a hypocrite. My conduct doesn't match what I claim to believe.

Feelings do not enter the equation.

Let's pause to absorb this idea.

Our feelings do not make us hypocrites. Only our words and actions do.

This leads to the question: when might our words and actions not coincide in our spiritual lives?

As Christians, we subscribe to the belief that God is the standard for right and anything that falls short of His perfection is therefore wrong. The ideal is Jesus, revealed to us through God's Word.

A key characteristic of a Christian is his or her pledge to follow Christ and His teachings. That's what baptism is all about—it's a formal declaration of this spiritual decision.

This means that anything in a Christian's life that does not match God's perfection could be construed as hypocritical. We have decided to submit ourselves to Him and obey His Word. We *say* we believe, but what do we *do*? If we rebel, we are hypocrites based on our own declaration.

"Wait a minute," someone may say. "None of us is perfect. None of us can follow Jesus without sin or mistakes 100 percent of the time. Does this mean we're all hypocrites?"

Perhaps. But maybe the best answer lies in our response to another question: What is our goal? What are we focussed on?

Hypocrisy doesn't enter into the equation if we are truly living lives submitted to Christ—if following Him is our consistent target, even when we sometimes fail to achieve it.

Why, then, were the Pharisees condemned?

Their aim was to gain honour from men rather than from God. In their case, hypocrisy was a legitimate charge. They *said* they were seeking God, yet their *focus* was not on Him but on man.

If we say we believe in Jesus, and if our wholehearted focus is on Him and on following Him, we are not hypocrites. We are not claiming to be without sin but are simply trying to live humble and obedient lives.

Let's return to our fallacy. Is forgiveness a feeling? Where does this leave a decision to forgive, even when we don't feel like forgiving? What is the right and authentic approach?

As genuine Christians, we choose to follow Jesus. We allow Him to have the influence that we *say* He has. If we call Him 'Lord' in our prayers—and that word means 'master'—then in integrity, we must treat Him as the One who has authority over our everything.

Forgiveness, even when we don't feel like extending it, is not hypocritical. We don't let fickle feelings rule us. When we forgive, we are doing what we say we will do. We are following Christ.

Fallacy #2: We have to forget to forgive.

It's not uncommon for religion to influence language and culture. This happens around the world. North American countries were founded by Bible-believing people, so the Bible tends to be embedded in our fundamental concepts. In non-Western countries, other religions, like Confucianism or Islam, are often the foundations of society. In Japan, a culture influenced by Buddhist principles, Buddhist idioms are frequently used.

I find it fascinating to observe what happens as a culture moves away from its underpinnings. When fewer and fewer people believe—truly believe—and practice the base cultural religion, common idioms and phrases begin to shift. Since most people no longer study the original teachings, sayings morph into something slightly different.

In Western culture, we often hear the phrase 'money is the root of all evil'. Some may recognize that this saying comes from the Bible—and they would be right, sort of. The actual verse says, "*the love of* money is the root of all evil" (1 Timothy 6:10, KJV, emphasis mine). That's quite different from the common, morphed statement.

It's interesting, isn't it? When we sit down and think about the modified version, it seems a little nonsensical:

- If money causes all evil, then surely the poor must always be good. After all, they have no money.
- How can something inanimate—like coins—cause corruption?
- How can something that can fund praiseworthy things—like hospitals, education, and charity for the poor—be the *root* of all evil?

When we examine the *love* of money as the root of all evil, it takes less imagination to see this is true. Such love is not limited to the wealthy. At times, a poor man may love money more than a rich one does. The love of money can lead to greed, coveting belongings of others, stinginess, idolatry (i.e., worshipping money), materialism, cheating, stealing, fraud, and other evils that may escalate. These things subvert the causes of good.

Misremembering the original phrase removes the Bible's valuable warning about the perils of an ungodly and idolatrous attitude. We should be cautious about allowing our culture to define our biblical knowledge. It's easy to miss a word or two when memorizing or quoting Scripture. This is why it's vital to continually reread the Scriptures, to check that our memories are correct and that the teachings of our pastors and leaders are biblically sound. We don't want to become propagators of false doctrines.

Another phrase commonly thought to be biblical is 'forgive and forget'. Though this line is quoted often in Western culture, it is not actually in the Bible. The Scriptures issue no instruction to forgive and forget. There is only the command to forgive—and we will examine it soon. For now, let's concentrate on the damaging fallacy that forgiving requires forgetting.

Several years ago, I heard a pastor talk about the phrase 'forgive and forget' as if it were in the Bible. A few days later, I discussed this with a friend. She turned to me with wild-eyed futility.

"I've been trying to forgive someone who wronged me, but I can't forget what she did!"

This poor woman was beside herself. She didn't know how to get past her inability to forget so she could obey God's command to forgive. When I showed her forgetting was not a prerequisite to forgiving, she was relieved.

When we forgive someone, we do not automatically forget the wrongs we've endured. This requirement is not biblical, so let us dispense with that lie right here.

It's true that eventually our memories fade, and we may forget the sharpness of the distress we experienced earlier, but it's important to treat our hurt selves and feelings with dignity and compassion. We can't afford to orphan or abandon that part of ourselves. This process is not so much about forgetting as about gaining freedom, through forgiveness, from past injuries and injustices.

Fallacy #3: Forgiveness makes excuses and lets the other person off the hook.

Let's get something straight. Forgiveness doesn't let anyone off the hook but ourselves. Without it, we are irrevocably tied to the person who has wronged us. With it, we can experience unparalleled joy and healing and peace.

Forgiveness does not mean what was done to injure us was acceptable.

I've noticed an interesting trend in the recent verbiage of our society when forgiving others. People may respond to an apology with, "That's okay, it's not your fault" even when the other person is blatantly guilty.

This phrasing is disingenuous to our emotional reality. It minimizes our pain and diminishes the wrong. When wounded, we need our distress to be acknowledged as valid both by ourselves and by the offender. Minimizing suffering short circuits our own healing process.

It also makes forgiveness less robust.

For instance, imagine I have wronged a friend. She has 'forgiven' me with the words, "That's okay, it's not your fault."

But I know the hurt *was* my fault. Do I feel confident in my friend's forgiveness? Perhaps our relationship is less strained—for now. But my friend has not acknowledged my guilt. I may not recognize it consciously, but now uncertainty weakens our bond. One of the key components of forgiveness lies in considering the offending party *guilty* and forgiving that person anyway.[8]

Time wears on, and my uneasiness increases.

What if my friend later realizes I *am* to blame? Will her forgiveness still hold?

This question may haunt our relationship.

Renowned theologian C.S. Lewis once mused, "If one is not really to blame, then there is nothing to forgive. In that sense forgiveness and excusing are almost opposites." As Martin Luther King Jr. put it, if we have been wronged, forgiveness "does not mean ignoring what has been done or putting a false label on an evil act. It means, rather, that the evil act no longer remains as a barrier to the relationship."[9]

Forgiveness doesn't whitewash sin. It admits that sin is hideous and destructive. What was done was wrong, and we bow our heads and mourn for what has been lost. Without properly recognizing sin and wrongdoing for what they are, we cannot experience redemption.[10]

Let's look again at the life of Jesus. He first had to acknowledge our sin for what it was before paying the ultimate price and dying on the cross to forgive us and transform us into whole and healthy people. If He had to do this—and He is God!—what makes us think we can bypass this necessary step? After all, we were made in His image.

Christian apologist and evangelist Josh McDowell provides a wonderful illustration in his book, *More Than a Car-*

penter. Suppose I go to a friend's house and, being the klutz I am, knock over his lamp.

It shatters on the floor.

I'm distraught at my clumsiness and offer to purchase a replacement. I apologize profusely.

My gracious friend says, "It's okay, I forgive you. You don't have to pay for it. I'll get another one later."

I am forgiven. I no longer have to worry about uncertainty in our relationship.

But here's the thing: forgiveness always comes with a cost. My friend would have been well within his rights to accept my offer of reimbursement. He didn't, but that doesn't mean the expense just disappears. He will bear it himself. He will be the one to purchase the new lamp. His graciousness has cost him something.

As American pastor and writer Warren Wiersbe once put it, "Mature Christians understand that forgiveness is not a cheap exchange of words, the way squabbling children often flippantly say 'I'm sorry' to each other. True forgiveness always involves pain; somebody has been hurt and there is a price to pay in healing the wound."[11]

Fallacy #4: I have to forgive only if someone has sinned against me.

Martin Luther King Jr. once wrote, "Forgiveness is not an occasional act, it's a permanent attitude." This mentality isn't required only when someone has sinned against us. Bitterness can crop up at any time in our relationships. Sometimes it can sprout out of jealousy or other emotions that have nothing to do with another person's behaviour. Like poison, it can spread through our spiritual selves, twisting them until they're misshapen and ugly.

The Bible repeatedly addresses the subject of bitterness. Hebrews 12:14–15 says, "Pursue peace with all men…see to it that no one comes short of the grace of God; that no root of bitterness springing up causes trouble." It's easy to see that bitterness can cause problems leading to many other sins, like gossip and hatred. For this reason, the apostle Paul wrote, "Let all bitterness and wrath and anger and clamor and slander be put away from you, along with all malice" (Ephesians 4:31).

If bitterness is a poison, then forgiveness is its antidote. Forgiveness sucks out the venom from our spiritual bloodstream and allows the Holy Spirit to whisper His tender love and mercy not only to our spirits but also to those of others—through us.

Perceptions shape our reality. Many years ago, a doctor prescribed a powerful medication for me. My body has never done well with side effects; every drug I've taken but one has caused some negative reaction. This new medication was no exception. It altered my perceptions. I started to think my boss was out to get me. As my thoughts became increasingly bizarre, I realized something was wrong. Thank goodness I had read the list of side effects before beginning this new treatment, or I might never have figured out it was giving me paranoid delusions. I stopped taking it immediately. Life returned to normal.

Not everyone has taken perception-altering medication. However, we all have our own points of view. If I think people are angry with me, my interactions with them will be different than if I think they're happy with me. Perceptions have immense power over our experience of reality.

Perception can heavily influence assumption. In our daily lives, we have to make fact-based assumptions in order to function. The sun has risen every day throughout recorded history. This is a fact. I don't need to know or understand the scientific causes to recognize this. If we didn't assume the sun would come up tomorrow or the ground would hold our weight, we wouldn't be able to go about our lives normally. We would be immobilized, perpetually questioning everything and unable to make new discoveries or inventions.

We make assumptions about people, their behaviour, and their motives. These may be accurate, but sometimes they may contain flaws. When we've held a premise for a long time, we may forget its origin and start treating it like a fact. Then we build another conjecture on the 'facts' and another. Soon, if we're not careful, we end up with a shaky tower of reasoning indeed! Perhaps it starts to resemble the Leaning Tower of Pisa. It might threaten to tumble at any second.

I've found that one of the key ingredients in living a humble and godly lifestyle is to frequently re-evaluate my assumptions about God and people, submitting them to the authority of the Scriptures and the Holy Spirit. Obviously, we don't constantly question and re-question Jesus' work on the cross and our own salvation. These things are facts, not suppositions. But what about our belief that we are successfully following and obeying God right now? What about our negative conjectures about the people around us?

Sometimes we need to forgive people for not living up to our expectations, and sometimes we need to forgive them for making mistaken inferences about us. We may not have been truly wronged in either case, but that does not preclude the need for forgiveness so the poison of bitterness doesn't creep in.

When we allow the Holy Spirit to tenderly probe our hearts, when we open ourselves to His gentle conviction, amazing things can happen. There is nothing so infused with godly humility as the statement, "I could be wrong."

Once, when a co-worker mistreated me, his deeds were discovered, and he was penalized for his wrongdoing. I forgave him, but he wanted nothing to do with me. He rejected the reconciliation I offered.

In trying to understand what was going on, I discussed the situation with my mother.

"I've forgiven him, but something seems off. I know I've done nothing wrong, but it's almost as though he needs to forgive me somehow."

"Sometimes we need to forgive even if there has been no sin against us," she said. "There is such a thing as having to forgive someone for being right."

Fallacy #5: I need an apology before I can forgive.

The Bible tells us God initiated the process of forgiveness while we were still His enemies. We offered Him no apology beforehand. This demonstrates that forgiveness can be one-sided. It doesn't require the offender to experience remorse, offer repentance, or make amends. The person who has suffered has the unilateral choice of whether to forgive. It's up to the recipient to decide whether to accept the forgiveness and move on towards a healthy, healed relationship.

In his book *Why Forgive?* J.C. Arnold recounts the story of Bill Chadwick, whose son was killed by a drunken driver. Bill embarked on an arduous emotional journey.

"I had to be willing to forgive without the score being even," Chadwick said. "This process of forgiveness did not really involve the driver—it involved me. I had to change, no matter what he did."[12]

Our Saviour well knows the pain of such a process. Luke 23 tells the poignant story, which I've rephrased here:

> Jesus is in agony, dying on the cross. He looks at the people gathered to watch Him die.

There are His disciples at the back, their leader being publicly mocked and executed while they stand at a distance, hearts breaking along with their dreams.

There are the Pharisees, gloating with the demons over their victory.

There are the rest of the people, the multitudes who once hung on his every word and deed, now watching Him hang from this accursed plank.

And there are the Roman soldiers, playing dice at the foot of His cross, gambling for the clothing they tore from His body before driving metal spikes through His hands and feet.

Every breath costs Him. Jesus pushes His feet against the cross. For an instant, His airways open. Lightning bolts of pain crackle up His legs.

Inhale.

This breath is precious. He's paid a price for this puff of air, and He plans to use it for something more precious still.

"Father, forgive them."

He turns to the soldiers. There is the one who spit in His face. The one who tugged the purple robe onto His shredded back. The one who wielded the whip with its vicious, metallic shards.

"Father, forgive them, for they know not what they do."

The soldiers never apologized, but Jesus asked His Father to forgive them. He would not have asked His Father for this without first having forgiven them Himself. Without first forgiving those who have wronged us, we won't ask other people to forgive them. That's human nature. This implies Jesus had already forgiven the soldiers, without their apology, when He prayed to His Father.

I have some personal experience with this concept and its application.

I was eighteen before I finally told my parents about the sexual abuse I had experienced. By then, it had been over for about a decade. The ragged claw marks on my soul had been hemorrhaging for a long time.

I still remember the horror, helplessness, and fury in the room when I told my mother and father.

Though the neighbourhood boy who abused me had used fear and manipulation to control me, over the ensuing years God had somehow enabled me to start the forgiveness process. I could reach out to my parents in their pain and help them begin to forgive as well. This never would have been possible if I hadn't already decided to forgive that boy myself. Helping my parents was proof that forgiveness was present in my own heart.

Though people can't *receive* forgiveness without first repenting, we can choose to forgive them even if they're remorseless.

Forgiveness may be free, but it demands payment beyond money. It requires a sacrifice to extend it and a sacrifice—of our own pride—to receive it.

6
What Forgiveness Is

> *She was busy thinking about the concept of forgiveness. It was such a lovely, generous idea when it wasn't linked to something awful that needed forgiving.*
>
> LIANE MORIARTY, *WHAT ALICE FORGOT*

ONE DAY, A JAPANESE FRIEND approached me with questions about forgiveness. After clarifying what it wasn't, I found myself struggling to explain what it was! I had to go away, think about it, and get back to her with a clearer answer.

My dictionary defines the verb 'to forgive' as:

- to grant pardon for an offense;
- to give up all claim on account of;
- to cease to feel resentment against; and
- to cancel an indebtedness or liability.[1]

That's just in English. Having lived abroad for several years, I've found that the definition and understanding of common human experiences differs by culture.[2] These varied descriptions offer a valuable opportunity to dig into the mentalities of other civilizations and enrich our own understanding of foundational experiences.

The definition of forgiveness in English differs from the definitions in the biblical languages. The Hebrew of the Old Testament uses the verb *nasa*, which means "to carry, bear away or lift up the faults, sins and failures of others—to consider them guilty but forgiven."[3] In Greek, some of the most frequent New Testament terms are *aphiemi*, "the concept of the unmerited forgiveness,"[4] and *charizomai*, "meaning 'to extend grace'."[5]

Unlike the English idea of settling accounts, biblical words imply some sort of responsibility for bearing the burden of others' faults away from them and a recognition that the offending parties cannot earn such a gift.

When we forgive someone, we no longer feel that person owes us something. Yes, we've been injured, but there's no longer a debt to be repaid. 'Wronged person' is not stamped on our souls as part of our identity. Forgiveness fosters emotional healing. When this happens, the thought of injustice no longer wakes us up in the middle of the night, takes away our appetite, or drives our lust for revenge.

Definitions can only tell part of the story. Relational concepts, such as love, forgiveness, and grace, require demonstration. That's why God didn't just *tell* us what love is. He sent an example through His Son, Jesus.

Let's conduct another thought scenario. Suppose we've been hurt by Mr. Albert Unforgiven. We are now struggling with the injustice that has occurred.

If we've been wronged, we tend to wish bad things upon Albert—or, at least, some sort of judgment by heavenly or earthly courts. We're also inclined to feel angry when good things happen to him. In a sense, we feel the injustice is compounded when Albert experiences joy and peace.

He doesn't deserve something good, we think. *That should be mine. Not only has he wronged me, now he's stealing the good things that belong to me!*

Alternatively, we may feel threatened when good things happen to Albert. We think they may enable him to cause further harm to us or others.

In any case, our sense of justice is injured every time something positive happens to Mr. Unforgiven.

When we forgive, Albert Unforgiven goes through a name change. He's now Bertie Forgiven. His identity in our minds' eye is transformed. We are readier to appreciate his good qualities and see the other side of who he is. We no longer wish bad things upon Bertie, and we no longer perceive threats in the good things.

But it doesn't end there. If it did, the criteria for forgiveness could be synonymous with those for indifference or disowning someone. Most of us know instinctively that this is not the best form of forgiveness. This is not the sort we would wish to receive ourselves, were we in the wrong. True forgiveness goes one step further. It hopes for *good* to those who have hurt us. It's not cold and indifferent. It loves.

7

How Forgiveness Changed the World

The cruelest prison of all is the prison of an unforgiving mind and spirit.

JOHANN CHRISTOPH ARNOLD, AUTHOR AND PASTOR

THE PASTOR AT MY CHILDHOOD church, like many pastors across North America, was fond of telling this story in his sermons:

> There once was a man taking vacation by the sea. He liked to get up early and stroll along the beach, the tides lapping at his feet. One morning, he noticed a boy in the distance, flinging something with all his might into the water. As he got closer, he realized the lad was picking up starfish and throwing them back into the ocean.
>
> The futility of the task struck the man. He approached with a kind smile.
>
> "You know, there are so many starfish here," he started. "There's no way that tossing a few back into the water will make any difference. You should go and play instead."
>
> The boy hesitated. He scooped up a starfish and showed it to the man.

"It makes a difference to this one," he said.

Then the boy threw "this one" with all his might, back into the water.

Forgiveness transforms one person at a time. It may affect the heart of the forgiven, but it transforms the heart of the forgiver even more. When the enormity of the task threatens to shut us down, we need only remember that it matters to each life touched along the way.

Any discussion on how forgiveness changed the world must start with Jesus. His grace and salvation have made such a radical impact that every other contribution in history pales by comparison.

Because of Jesus' sacrifice, His followers have been commissioned to go out into the world and share good news and hope with people everywhere. Jesus' message has given value and dignity to all life, since it's established on principles of equality, freedom, and justice. The concepts of giving to those who can't pay us back, compassion, and charity for the helpless and oppressed have led to establishing orphanages, abolishing slavery and child labour, caring for the aged, providing government welfare, and volunteering. Servants of Jesus have established hospitals and education systems for all people, regardless of gender or ethnicity. Those who work for a living have been given dignity, property rights, and individual freedom. And of course, followers of Jesus have made massive contributions to art and architecture, science and mathematics, music and literature. The impact Jesus has had on our world is incalculable.[1]

People who call themselves Christians have also committed horrific atrocities. However, when they committed these evils, they were not obeying the Man who instructed His followers:

> Love your enemies, do good to those who hate you, bless those who curse you, pray for those who mistreat you. Whoever hits you on the cheek, offer him the other also; and whoever takes away your coat, do not withhold your shirt from him either. Give to everyone who asks of you, and whoever takes away what is yours, do not demand it back.
>
> LUKE 6:27–30

Those who follow Jesus' teachings have walked the way of peace, self-sacrifice, and martyrdom, not of war, brutality, and hatred. This provides external evidence of an incredible internal reality. Jesus' impact goes far deeper and wider than the visible world will ever show. His work on the cross has transformed lives, both big and small. It effected miraculous physical, emotional, and spiritual healing, and has enabled people to share with others the same forgiveness they have received. The lost are found, the blind can see, and the chains of sin and death fall away. These heart transformations have led to the other changes that Jesus' followers have helped bring about in this world.

It all starts with His mercy, extended to us. Without it, nothing else is possible. While Jesus was dying, He still had forgiveness on His mind. On the cross, He promised the thief beside Him that he would be with Him that day in Paradise. On the cross, He asked His Father to forgive the soldiers who were at that very moment torturing and killing Him.

Christians, who have been forgiven so much, should be willing to forgive much. People throughout history have allowed Christ's forgiveness to shape theirs, and it has changed the world. Let's look at a few examples.

Jim and Elisabeth Elliot

Jim and Elisabeth met while they were students at Wheaton College, a Christian university in Illinois. After five years of marriage, Jim made his final trip to Ecuador to pursue his dream of bringing Jesus' good news to the Huaorani people. He had been working for some time with four men to cultivate connections with the isolated tribe.[2]

On the visit just before their last, a cultural misunderstanding led the Huaorani people to believe the missionaries should be executed.[3]

Roger Youderian, Pete Fleming, Jim Elliot, Nate Saint, and Ed McCully were speared to death in January 1956, their bodies left floating in the Curaray river.

Horror rippled through the Christian community. No one felt the loss more keenly than the families of the slain men. Soon, however, the wives banded together. Not wanting their husbands' sacrifice to be wasted, they forgave the Huaorani people and approached them again with the good news of Jesus. Elisabeth Elliot, along with a few others, went to live with the Huaorani. She would spend more than two years there, as a missionary.

During that time, many of the Huaorani people became Christians. They now have a restored relationship with God because these women chose to courageously forgive. Because of them, members of a formerly unreached people will be in heaven at the end of time. Because of them, the faith of countless Christians around the world—including the famous theologian Chuck Swindoll[4]—has also been challenged and deepened.

Martin Luther King Jr.

Born the son of a famous Black American preacher, Martin Luther King Jr. received a commission from God—to stand up for righteousness, justice, and truth in the face of racism and hatred. "That inner voice...the voice of Jesus," King later said, "promised never to leave me, no, never to leave me alone."[5] That was a defining moment—one that would shape the rest of his life.[6]

King was a steadfast crusader for justice and equality, using nonviolent resistance. This he learned from another great man who was influenced by the life and teachings of Jesus, Mahatma Gandhi. For King's efforts, he endured bombings, assaults, stabbings, death threats, imprisonment, and all manner of violence against himself and those he loved. Nevertheless, he resolutely intended to follow his God-given mission.

His nonviolent tactics exposed racism for what it is, putrid and repugnant—an offense to everything we *say* we believe in. He challenged people to examine—even if it was only for an instant—whether their beliefs and attitudes matched their actions. In the end, masses of people steeped in racism from the womb got a jarring glimpse of themselves mirrored in the hate-filled faces of people on their television screens.[7]

His aim was not to change a few *laws* but to have a lasting impact on people's *hearts*. He didn't want outward hypocrisy with hearts still full of hate. He wanted radical racial reconciliation.

How could this be his desire for people whose goal was to silence him by any means necessary? King adopted an attitude of forgiveness that fed his drive towards nonviolence and his desire for God's best to all humankind—whether or not they hated him. He was out not for revenge but for love.

"We love men not because we like them," he once wrote, "nor because their ways appeal to us, nor even because they possess some kind of divine spark. We love every man because God loves him."[8]

Eventually, King was assassinated for his crusade. But the inroads he made against racism in the American Civil Rights movement would far outlast his earthly lifespan.

Corrie ten Boom

Corrie ten Boom and her family were captured by the Nazis during World War II. For helping Jews and those involved in resistance activities to escape, Corrie and her family were sent to a concentration camp.[9]

They endured great hardship. Corrie suffered the agony of watching her beloved sister, Betsie, wither before her eyes. In the end, Corrie was the only member of her family to survive the Holocaust.

Following the war, she wrote dozens of books. Corrie's stories and insights soon made her famous. She went on speaking tours around the world, sharing about her sister and the way Jesus can transform our suffering into joy through the forgiveness He offers to and through us.

One evening, her message was tested most dramatically. Here is the story, in her words.

> It was at a church service in Munich that I saw him, the former S.S. man who had stood guard at the shower room door in the processing center at Ravensbrück. He was the first of our actual jailers that I had seen since that time. And suddenly it was all there—the roomful of mocking men, the heaps of clothing, Betsie's pain-blanched face.
>
> He came up to me as the church was emptying, beaming and bowing.

"How grateful I am for your message, *Fraulein*." he said. "To think that, as you say, He has washed my sins away!"

His hand was thrust out to shake mine. And I, who had preached so often to the people in Bloemendaal the need to forgive, kept my hand at my side.

Even as the angry, vengeful thoughts boiled through me, I saw the sin of them. Jesus Christ had died for this man; was I going to ask for more? *Lord Jesus*, I prayed, *forgive me and help me to forgive him.*

I tried to smile, I struggled to raise my hand. I could not. I felt nothing, not the slightest spark of warmth or charity. And so again I breathed a silent prayer. *Jesus, I cannot forgive him. Give Your forgiveness.* As I took his hand the most incredible thing happened. From my shoulder along my arm and through my hand, a current seemed to pass from me to him, while into my heart sprang a love for this stranger that almost overwhelmed me.[10]

Do you think the former guard ever found out Corrie was one of his previous victims?

I think so. If what she'd said had affected him so deeply, he probably bought one or two of her books in the ensuing years. Maybe he read the story above in her best-known book, *The Hiding Place*.

Do you think Corrie's forgiveness was significant to him?

I would imagine that apart from God's, hers was the opinion that mattered most.

I don't know what happened to the man after that meeting, but I do know what happened to me when I read that story. If Corrie, a Holocaust survivor, could forgive then so could I. God could enable me to impart supernatural forgiveness to the people who had wounded and abused me. I needed only the willingness to obey.

Millions of other people realized the same thing. Corrie ten Boom's sacrifice of forgiveness echoes on.

8

How Forgiveness Changes the World for Us

> *As we forgive, we find that not only do our own wounds heal, but our experience becomes the source of healing knowledge and power for others.*
>
> LEANNE PAYNE, FOUNDER OF *PASTORAL CARE MINISTRIES*

SOME STORIES, LIKE THOSE IN the previous chapter, dazzle us. We often consider the Christians involved as giants of faith. But what about the average, lesser-known person? How can forgiveness change the world for people like us?

CHRIS CARRIER, THE BOY WHO RESCUED HIS CAPTOR

Ten-year-old Chris Carrier was walking home from school at the start of Christmas holidays when a man approached him, claiming to be his father's friend. David McAllister asked for help with some party supplies. The boy agreed.

Chris was then abducted, stabbed, and shot in the head before being left for dead in a park. A local hunter later found his body.[1]

Though he escaped brain damage, Chris's life was marred by daily struggles with physical limitations and fear. His attacker was still out there somewhere.

Eventually, Chris came to terms with the trauma he had endured. He completed university and graduate school, married, and had children of his own.

Twenty-two years later, police contacted Chris with the news that someone had confessed to the attack. It turned out that McAllister had once been employed and terminated by the Carrier family, but there had never been sufficient evidence to prosecute him. Now he was dying.

Chris went to visit his attacker at a nursing home the day after he received the news. The sight that met his eyes was pitiful—a frail, elderly man, blind for several years, with no people or possessions of his own.

When the man apologized for all he had done, Chris's heart overflowed with compassion. He visited David many times over the following days—often accompanied by his wife and daughters.

He found himself repeating words from the Bible to his onetime captor: "You meant evil against me, but God meant it for good" (Genesis 50:20, ESV).

David's heart softened as time rolled by, and the two became friends. The last three weeks of McAllister's life were marked not by violence, not by frailty, but by friendship. After his death, the media reported on Chris and David's story.

They couldn't understand how Chris could forgive his abductor. Here's what Chris said:

> There is a very pragmatic reason for forgiving. When we are wronged, we can either respond by seeking revenge, or we can forgive. If we choose revenge, our lives will be consumed by anger. When vengeance is served, it leaves one empty. Anger is a hard urge to satisfy and can become habitual. But forgiveness allows us to move on.[2]

"You tricked me!" you may say. "Chris isn't normal. You promised to tell me about how forgiveness can change the world for *normal* people."

But that's the point. This story reminds us that Jesus' forgiveness changes the mundane into the extraordinary. There are no 'normal' stories.

Chris started out as a typical ten-year-old boy, faced with a horror. What he did with it was life changing. Now he presents a challenge to others—to follow with him in the footsteps of Jesus.

The Amish, who practiced what they preached

Charles Roberts IV drove a milk truck, making deliveries to people in an Amish community. He was married and had three children.[3]

On the last day of his life, he walked his kids to the bus stop with his wife,[4] then went to an Amish school, armed with an assortment of guns.[5] He told the teacher and boys to leave the classroom and bound the legs of the girls. He shot them all before turning the gun on himself.

Over the following days, fragments of Charles' story were released. His infant daughter had passed away several years earlier; one of his suicide notes indicated he was angry at God.[6] His messages were confusing, and no one knows why Charles did what he did. However, the destruction he left in his wake was undeniable. Five little girls died, and the rest were hospitalized.

Then something remarkable happened. The Amish community gathered around Charles' widow and children within hours. Members reached out in compassion and asked after the family. One person started a food drive. On the day of Charles' funeral, about half the mourners were from the families of his victims.

"All religions teach forgiveness," said one TV reporter. "But no one really does it, like the Amish are trying to do. What is the difference?"[7]

The Amish are not so different from you and me. They experience the same lusts and passions, temptations and failures as all people do. The difference did not lie in their lifestyle. It lay in the Person they were obeying. Jesus Christ is the answer. He is the One who enables us to forgive not only those who hurt us but also those who hurt our loved ones.

Jean-Paul Samputu, the singer who became an instrument of grace

Jean-Paul Samputu was a Rwandan singer who gave concerts around the world—from Africa to America and everywhere in between. His father told him to flee Rwanda in 1994 during the genocide. He toured Africa and returned to his country that July.[8]

The killing had ended by then. His parents, three of his brothers, and his sister were dead. Survivors in his hometown told him that Vincent, his best friend from childhood, had murdered his mother and father.

Anger and pain became Jean-Paul's reality. In his heart, war was still raging. He used alcohol and drugs to numb himself. Continually drunk, soon he could no longer perform at concerts. His Ugandan friends tried to help by taking him to a witch doctor for an exorcism. Nothing worked.

He and his wife moved to Canada in 1998. Two years later, Jean-Paul left her and went back to Uganda, where he was still famous. He repeatedly ended up in prison.

Then he visited his brother in Kenya. There he met a Christian named Moses, who said God had instructed him to find Jean-Paul and pray for him. Though skeptical, Jean-Paul allowed this.

In his prayers, Moses commanded demons to leave Jean-Paul alone. Whenever Moses said the name of Jesus, Jean-Paul felt strange. Sometimes he would collapse. At other times, he would vomit. He recognized the power in those prayers.

"You are the best of the witch doctors," Jean-Paul told him.[9]

"I am not a witch doctor," Moses said. "I won't provide you with healing. Jesus will."

Jean-Paul would come to know and love this Jesus over the coming months.

Three years later, he went on a months-long pilgrimage to a Ugandan mountain to pray. Night after night God gave him the same inescapable message: "You must forgive."

Outwardly, Jean-Paul was no longer dependent on alcohol or drugs. Inwardly, his heart was still full of bitterness. This yielded a different, more insidious dependency. He struggled against God's command for a year. He knew that were he to give in, he would have to forgive Vincent and ask others for forgiveness too.

Finally, he relented.

"I'm ready to forgive Vincent," he said aloud to himself one day. God healed and freed him from everything in his past in an instant.

Jean-Paul discovered that his former friend was in jail. He sent news of his forgiveness through Vincent's wife. Vincent didn't believe it at first and thought Jean-Paul was trying to trick him for some nefarious purpose. Before Jean-Paul's transformation, such a suspicion would have been well-founded.

When Vincent expressed disbelief, his wife told him, "I have talked with Samputu. If you don't accept his forgiveness, that's your problem. But let me tell you one thing. It's not *him* who's forgiving you. It's God. It's grace."[10]

When Vincent accepted his friend's forgiveness, an amazing thing happened. Vincent's entire family forgave him, and they were reunited.

The healing didn't stop there. In 2005, Jean-Paul returned to Canada. He also reconciled with his wife and children.

To this day, Jean-Paul maintains contact with Vincent, his old friend. And every time he's in the area, he goes to Vincent's house and eats with the family.

Charles Williams, whose eyes were changed

Charles Williams grew up in a small town in New York state, with a violent, alcoholic mother. His childhood years were nightmarish. By the time he reached adulthood, he was addicted to anger over the past. This had a profound effect on his other relationships. His marriage and parenting suffered.[11]

He realized that to be free of his former life he needed to forgive his mother. It took him five years to build up the resolve to take the next step. Then he visited her.

"I can tell you one thing—it wasn't easy," Charles says. "On the other hand, this person in front of me—this person who was, in my mind's eye, a crazed monster with a wild look in her eyes—instantaneously changed into a frail, sickly, old woman on oxygen, dying of emphysema. She became the mother I had never had."[12]

That's exactly what forgiveness does—it changes the eyes of our hearts, so we see those we've forgiven in a different light.

Valerie Limmer, whose God defied the odds

In my own childhood, I encountered abuse—physical, sexual, and emotional—at the hands of two adults and an older child.

The statistics say I will be emotionally unhealthy, that I am most likely married to someone who will be abusive, and that I will probably perpetuate that abuse to others.

The statistics are wrong.

In our adult lives, for a time my husband and I suffered horrendous verbal, spiritual, and emotional abuse. Each therapist we talked with afterward said the same thing—they were amazed we weren't destroyed by the experience.

But we forgave those who hurt us while they were still hurting us. God honoured our submission and, over time, He healed us. At times, our wounds resurface, and we continue to forgive.

When we take hold of the power of God and courageously decide to step forward in faith, statistics don't matter. God is more powerful. He will honour our obedience and change our reality to be something far beyond—and far better than—anything we could have imagined.

Sometimes He heals us fully, at once. Other times, He takes us on a journey of restoration that lasts our whole lives. Whatever the case, the destination is always healing, and the journey is always worth it.

Closing Part II
Food for Thought

AFTER GOD ENABLED CORRIE TEN BOOM to forgive the soldier who had worked at the camp where her sister died, she would write, "I discovered that it is not on our forgiveness any more than on our goodness that the world's healing hinges, but on His. When He tells us to love our enemies, He gives, along with the command, the love itself."[1]

God never commands us to do something that He does not also enable us to do. We need only the resolve to obey. Remembering God's forgiveness can help bolster our own; our response of love and gratitude spurs us on. Jesus' teaching still holds true today; those who have been forgiven much are those who love much.

The Bible says, "Love never fails" (1 Corinthians 13:8). The undertone of this phrase in the original language is that love never fails to make an impact. Love never fails to make a mark.[2] When we remember that we have been forgiven much, we love much. Those who love much can change the world.

Going Deeper

1. Write out your definition of forgiveness. Use clear language. Imagine talking to an adult from another country who can understand difficult concepts but not long words. Try to replace words greater than three syllables with simpler ones. Read over everything again. Fill the gaps in your thinking and clarify any ambiguities.

2. Why might forgiveness be an antidote to bitterness? Think through and explain how this antidote may work.

3. Is there any part of the forgiveness process, as described in the story of Albert Unforgiven, that is particularly difficult for you? Write a prayer asking God to enable you to go through this part of the process with someone who has wronged you.

4. Why do you think forgiveness can have such a profound impact—not only on those who forgive and are forgiven but also on those who hear stories of forgiveness?

5. How might the words of Joseph—"You meant evil against me, but God meant it for good" (Genesis 50:20, ESV)—help us forgive?

Part III

Our Foundation

JOHN WESLEY WAS BORN IN England and educated as an Anglican priest. One day, a member of British Parliament named James Oglethorpe approached him with a request. Would he be willing to make the arduous journey to the Colonies (now the United States) as a minister? Were he to accept, he would work with the people of Savannah, Georgia.

Accept Wesley did, and soon he was on his way to that new land. On the journey, the main mast of the sailing ship broke, and the lives of all on board were in peril. Wesley cowered at the prospect of looming death along with everyone else—well, almost everyone. A small group of passengers calmly prayed and sang hymns in the face of almost-certain demise.

How can they be so calm? Wesley wondered.

After the crisis had passed, Wesley befriended the group, who turned out to be Moravians. He discovered that the source of their inner strength was an intimate relationship with God, born of salvation through faith, which had been absent from his own life until then.[1] He would eventually embrace those same principles and establish the Methodist church.

Wesley later had a conversation with the man who had been instrumental in starting his journey of faith. Oglethorpe, known to be an inflexible man, boasted, "I never forgive."

"Well, sir," John Wesley responded, "then I hope you never sin."[2]

9
Who We Are

> *Consider your calling, brethren...*
> 1 Corinthians 1:26

A FEW CHARACTERISTICS ARE CENTRAL to our Christian identities. I like to think of them as our spiritual DNA, elements inseparable from our heritage as followers of Jesus and children of God. Let's examine the two most prominent ones here.

1. Unity

Jesus went to the garden of Gethsemane with His disciples after the Last Supper. He would be arrested there later that night. Before then, however, He prayed for His current followers and the future church.

> "I do not ask on behalf of these alone," He said, "but for those also who believe in Me through their word; that they may all be one; even as You, Father, are in Me and I in You, that they also may be in Us, so that the world may believe that You sent Me...and loved them, even as You have loved Me."
>
> John 17:20–21, 23

Jesus prayed for unity among His followers. He asked that they would all be one. He mentioned His own relationship with His Father and its characteristic unity as the pattern He desired for all His people. That's what it means to follow Jesus. We want to watch and copy Him, just as children watch and copy their parents.

Notice the reason for this desire. It's for the sake not only of Jesus' followers but also for the welfare of those who don't yet know Him. We are to be unified so the world will trust that God the Father sent Jesus, and so it will know of His love.

Let's pause on that truth for a moment.

- How can people come to accept the significance of Jesus' death, resurrection, and salvation without first believing He had a divine purpose?

- How can they open up to God the Father unless they also believe He sent Jesus to earth as the One who would reconcile all humankind to Himself?

- How can they trust in His salvation without knowing He loves them?

The Great Commission—the foundational mission statement of every Christian since Jesus returned to heaven on the clouds—cannot be fulfilled without oneness between believers. Absent this unity, our whole purpose as Jesus' disciples is lost.

Many of us have become socially stingy, unwilling to invest in mending relationships when conflicts flare up. We embrace the mentality that if things don't work out, we can always discard our friendship du jour and pick up another one. This is the same attitude adopted by people who are not Christians. Such secular beliefs have also seeped into the minds of Christians.

In his letter to the Roman church, the apostle Paul wrote, "May the God of endurance and encouragement grant you to live in such harmony with one another, in accord with Christ Jesus" (Romans 15:5, ESV).

Did you get that? Living in harmony with one another requires endurance. It is not always convenient. We need to adopt a mindset and habit of persistence that will endure through those times when difficulties hurt our relationships.

There's no way to say this too strongly: a discard-and-replace mentality is unhealthy and destructive. It's harmful not only to us but also to God's reputation.[1] For those who don't believe in Jesus, Christian disunity proves God the Father did not send Jesus and that He does not love them.

When we Christians are not unified, we become living proof *against* our Saviour.

2. Love

We are limited beings interacting with an infinite God. We cannot fully grasp many aspects of our faith—not now and perhaps not ever. We don't need to master every detail of

Jesus' marvellous salvation to believe its larger truths. That's what makes it so beautiful and wonderful: even a little child can absorb enough to enter Jesus' kingdom.

There is, however, one thing we absolutely must understand: the primacy of love in our Christian lives. The Scriptures speak to this.

"The one who does not love does not know God, for God is love." (1 John 4:8) One of our chief goals as Christians is to know and experience an intimate, continuous relationship with our heavenly Father. If God is love, then we must make love an integral part of our lives.

"Beloved, if God so loved us, we also ought to love one another." (1 John 4:11) This should not be surprising. It's along the same lines of the watching-and-copying we discussed earlier. If God is our heavenly Father, then we as His children should want to be like Him.

In His time on earth, Jesus said, *"A new commandment I give to you, that you love one another, even as I have loved you, that you also love one another. By this all men will know that you are My disciples, if you have love for one another." (John 13:34–35)*

Some families have certain prominent features that are common among the relatives. For some, it may be a distinctive nose. For others, it may be a high forehead or a type of jawline. For my mother, sister, and me, it's our eyes.

Spiritually, one distinguishing feature shows we all belong to the same family—our love. Without it, there is no way for the world to tell we are Jesus' disciples and part of His family. People who aren't Christians can still lead good lives outwardly. What sets us apart is our love.

"*Little children, let us not love with word or with tongue, but in deed and truth.*" *(1 John 3:18)* Jesus doesn't command loving lip service. No, we are to love with all our hearts. Words are easy. Loving in deed and truth—that's the hard part and that's the type of love He requires of us.

Lest we think we can love God without also loving our fellow human beings, the apostle John strips away that possibility.

"*If someone says, 'I love God,' and hates his brother, he is a liar; for the one who does not love his brother whom he has seen, cannot love God whom he has not seen.*" *(1 John 4:20)*

John later underscores what this entails: "*In fact, this is love for God: to keep his commands*" *(1 John 5:3, NIV).*

Remember what Jesus said? "*A new commandment I give to you, that you love one another.*" *(John 13:34)* If we don't obey Christ's command to love others, then we are not loving Him.

"Well, wait a minute," someone may say. "Christians have other attributes too. What if I don't have love, but I have abundant faith? Surely that's important! My faith will show I'm a part of God's family."

The apostle Paul puts all other Christian activities and characteristics into perspective: "*If I speak with the tongues of men and of angels, but do not have love, I have become a noisy gong or a clanging cymbal. If I have the gift of prophecy, and know all mysteries and all knowledge; and if I have all faith, so as to remove mountains, but do not have love, I am nothing. And if I give all my possessions to feed the poor, and if I surrender my body to be burned, but do not have love, it profits me nothing." (1 Corinthians 13:1–3)*

The 'love chapter' of 1 Corinthians 13 states, restates, and in case we missed it, states again that love is supreme. There is no higher calling; there is no greater thing. To put it simply, neither our faith nor our other actions matter if we don't have love.[2]

Pulling it all together

Here's the crux: practicing forgiveness is crucial to love and unity. Without forgiveness, we tend to have broken relationships. We hold grudges, harbour resentment, are tempted to gossip, and can't possibly remain unified when friction surfaces. When conflict comes to visit, love leaves the room. Conflict becomes that unwanted houseguest who never moves out.

The apostle Paul, in his famous soliloquy, lists several key attributes of love. One of them is "love keeps no record of wrongs" (1 Corinthians 13:5, NIV). A 'record of wrongs' is a little black book of all the things someone has ever done against you. Perhaps you keep it safe. Perhaps you keep it hidden. But in seasons of conflict, out it comes. In an argument with a friend, family member, or spouse, how many times have you or I recalled a hurt from another quarrel?

"Well, remember what you did to me?"

"You wronged me!"

Peter and I have a rule in our fights. Peter's better at following it than I am. Too often, I would rather dredge up things from the past to support my point of view. The principle is solid, though, so I try to follow it.

Here it is: we are never allowed to bring up something the other person has apologized for and that we've forgiven them for. What has been forgiven cannot later be used as a weapon. We aren't permitted pet grudges. We are not allowed to keep a record of wrongs.

There's something freeing about this. If "I forgive you" can't be taken back when it's inconvenient, then we can have deep confidence in our relationship. We don't have to be fearful of past faults coming back to haunt us. At times, we might experience consequences when one of us wrongs the other, but never punishment.

Repetitive sins, such as addiction or abuse, may require particular strategies for the good of both the victim and the victimizer. We will touch on some issues relevant to this later.

The Psalms assure us that God "has removed our sins as far from us as the east is from the west" (Psalm 103:12, NLT). When He forgives us, He remembers our sins against us no more. If we are to follow Him, we must do the same for others.

10

The Importance of Forgiveness

It is only with the heart that one can see clearly. The important things are invisible to the naked eye.

ANTOINE DE SAINT-EXUPÉRY, *THE LITTLE PRINCE*

JESUS OFTEN SHROUDED THE MEANING of His teachings in parables so that only those who earnestly sought the truth, who had "the ears to hear", would glean the fullest benefit from them. One day, He asked the multitude a question. "Why do you call Me, 'Lord, Lord,' and do not do what I say?" (Luke 6:46)

This question is quite ludicrous. The word 'Lord' means 'master'. In Jesus' day, it was a term a slave might have used when addressing his owner. Slaves lived in whatever conditions their masters saw fit to keep them. They had no say over their situations. They were property, and their masters could do whatever they wanted to them.

If you were a slave, when you were asked to do something, you did it. Right away. To the best of your ability. You did this because you had never known anything different. You had few personal rights and freedoms; all you knew was that if you served well, perhaps you would gain favour. You might be treated better. Perhaps you would receive more responsibility in the household and achieve a prestigious position.

Obedience with excellence was your only means of upward mobility. Unless your owner decided to give or sell you your freedom, you would always be a slave. Those who escaped would be hunted and beaten or killed. No one would help you get away. You would eventually be discovered, and the master would make an example of you to dissuade other slaves from trying to escape.

Some masters were kind; some were cruel. However, disobedience would incur consequences even from kind masters.

In the Jewish culture, repeating someone's name when addressing him or her indicated a special type of relational closeness.[1] That's what we see here. The repetition ("Lord, Lord") shows the master in this passage is kind. The slave feels relationally close to Him.

Perhaps the slave has let this intimacy go to his head. Yet, the Lord is still the master, and the slave should maintain an attitude of submission towards Him. This has not been the case. Somehow, the slave got too comfortable and discarded obedience. He lulled himself into complacency and placed himself in a shaky position. If other slaves see the disobedience tolerated, they will rebel too. The master must respond; the unruly slave is bringing himself perilously close to negative consequences.

In Matthew's version of this story, Jesus says, "Not everyone who says to me, 'Lord, Lord,' will enter the kingdom of heaven, but only the one who does the will of my Father who is in heaven" (Matthew 7:21, NIV).

Did you get that? Jesus is saying not everyone who feels close to Him will be allowed into the kingdom of heaven. Only those who do the will of His Father will enter.

Jesus tells a now-familiar story:

> Therefore everyone who hears these words of Mine and acts on them, may be compared to a wise man who built his house on the rock. And the rain fell, and the floods came, and the winds blew and slammed against that house; and yet it did not fall, for it had been founded on the rock. Everyone who hears these words of Mine and does not act on them, will be like a foolish man who built his house on the sand. The rain fell, and the floods came, and the winds blew and slammed against that house; and it fell—and great was its fall.
>
> MATTHEW 7:24–27

What made one man wise and the other foolish?
Perhaps one *came* to Jesus, but the other didn't?
No. Both men came.
Perhaps one *heard* Jesus' teaching, but the other didn't?
No. Both heard.
The difference was that the wise man *obeyed* Jesus' teaching after hearing it. The foolish man did not.
How careful we must be to not only listen to the words and teachings of Jesus but also to put them into practice!

Without obedience, we bring ourselves perilously close to our own destruction, like the unruly slave.

Jesus' warning still echoes today:

> Not everyone who says to me, 'Lord, Lord,' will enter the kingdom of heaven, but only the one who does the will of my Father who is in heaven.
>
> MATTHEW 7:21, NIV

This invites the question: how might we do the will of our Father in heaven? Jesus showed His disciples many things about leading lives that please and honour God. At one point, He taught them how to pray.

> "Our Father who art in heaven,
> Hallowed be Thy name,
> Thy kingdom come,
> Thy will be done,
> On earth as it is in heaven.
> Give us today our daily bread.
> And forgive us our debts,
> as we also have forgiven our debtors.
> And do not lead us into temptation,
> but deliver us from evil.
> For Thine is the kingdom,
> and the power, and the glory, forever.
> Amen."
>
> MATTHEW 6:9–13, NASB 1977

Notice that in this sample prayer, Jesus instructs us to ask our heavenly Father to forgive our sins. That seems pretty self-explanatory. Asking this of God is a staple of every Christian's life. But something else is mentioned here, something that *isn't* quite as common—it isn't, but it should be.

> And forgive us our debts,
> *as we also have forgiven* our debtors.
> MATTHEW 6:12, EMPHASIS MINE

If we're in any doubt, Jesus continues this teaching after He's finished praying.

"For if you forgive other people when they sin against you, your heavenly Father will also forgive you. But if you do not forgive others their sins, your Father will not forgive your sins." (Matthew 6:14–15, NIV)

Jesus makes our situation crystal clear; the forgiveness we extend to other people is linked to God's forgiveness of us.

We cannot afford to misunderstand this. The repercussions are too huge.

If we are unwilling to forgive others, God will not forgive us. In the words of the Puritans, "A man can as well go to hell for not forgiving as for not believing."[2]

This is counter to what we commonly understand about our faith today. After all, isn't it enough to believe in Jesus? Not according to the Bible. James 2:19 says, "You say you have faith, for you believe that there is one God. Good for you! Even the demons believe this, and they tremble in terror." (NLT) What makes us different from the demons? Our faith, demonstrated through obedience.

Human beings have been misunderstanding what it means to obey and forgive for eons. Jane Austen wrote several novels in the nineteenth century that remain popular to this day. In one of her best-known books, *Pride and Prejudice*, a character named Mr. Collins says, "You ought certainly to forgive them as a Christian, but never to admit them in your sight, or allow their names to be mentioned in your hearing." Some of us might tend to think he was right.

And yet, when we pray the Lord's Prayer, we ask God to forgive us in the same way we forgive others. Where would we be if He were to forgive us but decide never to admit us into His sight or allow our names to be mentioned in His hearing? Where would we be if this was God's definition of forgiveness?

> And forgive us our debts,
> *as we also have forgiven* our debtors.
> MATTHEW 6:12, EMPHASIS MINE

"This prayer is just a bunch of prewritten words on a page," someone may object. "Surely God won't hold me to them."

But why not? Can we not read? Do we not have the power and freedom to consider and choose what we say?

When the Jewish leaders attacked Jesus, He didn't chastise them for their unbelief. He told them they would be judged by the things they *said* they believed but didn't *follow*. Jesus lambasted the Pharisees for saying they believed in Moses but not taking his teachings to heart or applying the principles he taught.

"Do not think that I will accuse you before the Father," Jesus said. "The one who accuses you is Moses, in whom you have set your hope." (John 5:45)

During another face-off with the Pharisees, He said, "I tell you this, you must give an account on judgment day for every idle word you speak. The words you say will either acquit you or condemn you." (Matthew 12:36–37, NLT)

God will judge us in the same way. If the songs we sing, the prayers we pray, and the Scriptures we recite don't align with the things we do, our words will be the things that judge us. If our actions don't match our words, our own statements will convict us.

Can you hear the judge's gavel?

I can.

There I am, in two places at once, seated at the defense table at the end of time, staring at an earlier version of myself in the witness box. I'm incriminated by my own words.

When we recite the Lord's Prayer, we ask God to forgive us in the same way we forgive others. We would be wise to be cautious of praying it, then, if we are unwilling to forgive. As Charles Spurgeon once said, "Unless we have forgiven others, we read our own death warrant when we repeat the Lord's Prayer."[3]

11

Forgiveness Belongs to our God

My blood is poured out for many for forgiveness of sins.
Jesus, in Matthew 26:28

There's something remarkable about the relationship between love and forgiveness. When Jesus visited the house of a Pharisee named Simon, a woman came in, weeping. Seeing that her tears had splashed onto Jesus, she dried His feet with her hair and poured perfume on them.

Simon, observing this in horror, thought, *This woman is a sinner! No* decent *man would let her touch him. If Jesus were a prophet, He would recognize this!*

Knowing not only about the woman but also what was in Simon's heart, Jesus told a story to illustrate a singular concept.

> "A certain moneylender had two debtors: one owed five hundred denarii, and the other fifty. When they were unable to repay, he graciously forgave them both. Which of them therefore will love him more?"
>
> Luke 7:41–42

Jesus used this parable to chastise the Pharisees for their unloving approach. He compared Simon's poor hospitality to the grand treatment shown by the woman, who had poured expensive perfume on His feet. In the Middle East, showing a warm welcome is a prized social virtue, yet Jesus pointed out the holes in the Pharisee's reception in favour of that *sinful* woman's generosity!

"For this reason I say to you, her sins, which are many, have been forgiven," He said (Luke 7:47).

The Pharisees were indignant.

"Who is this man who even forgives sins?" According to the Jewish faith, only God could forgive iniquity. 'To err is human, to forgive, divine' is not a meaningless cliché. In the Jewish worldview, when Jesus forgave the woman's sins, He was declaring His own divinity.[1]

This story highlights a cyclical relationship; Jesus' love led Him to forgive the woman, and that forgiveness induced her to love Him. More broadly, love causes forgiveness, and forgiveness causes love. No wonder Christian writer and pastor J.C. Arnold wrote, "One of the most beautiful expressions of love is forgiving."

A fixation on judging others can limit our ability to learn. The Pharisees probably didn't hear much after Jesus forgave the woman's sins. They likely missed out on the richness of His teaching on the relationship between love and forgiveness. There's a reason Jesus often said, "Whoever has ears, let him hear." Too often we're focussed on something other than Him and miss what He has to teach us.

When you and I forgive, we become a little more like the people we were always meant to be—people created in God's image. How different from the 'eye for an eye' approach of the Old Testament, with its spotlight on justice and vengeance!

Yet even then, the fingerprints of God's compassion and forgiveness were apparent. During the time of Nehemiah, the Israelites were restored from their captivity back to the Promised Land. That generation had forgotten the old days, the ways of following God's laws. So, they held a public reading of the Scriptures. Then the Levites led the people in a time of communal repentance for their sinfulness. They reviewed their past disobedience and rebellion and remembered God's response with thankfulness.

> But You are a God of forgiveness,
> Gracious and compassionate,
> Slow to anger and abounding in lovingkindness;
> And You did not forsake our ancestors.
>
> NEHEMIAH 9:17

About a hundred years before Nehemiah lived, when the Israelites were still exiled from their homeland, the prophet Daniel also recognized God's character.

"To the Lord our God belong compassion and forgiveness," he wrote in Daniel 9:9.

Not only is Jehovah a God of forgiveness, but also forgiveness and compassion *belong* to Him. Let us never forget that our God prizes these things. There is no duality between the Old and New Testaments in this. The God of the Old Testament valued forgiveness and mercy so much that He sent His Son to proclaim those concepts through His life and death.

Our comprehension of these concepts has a dramatic impact on how we understand what it means to be the bride of Christ. One day I meditated on this in my devotions, using my journal as an aid.

We are the bride of Christ. What does this mean for our relationship with God? I wondered. *Why does He love us when we're so unhealthy? As a rule, an emotionally healthy person won't be attracted to an emotionally ill one. Is He unhealthy too, and we just don't know it?*

I remembered a time in my own life when I was emotionally ill. If my husband, Peter, had met me back then, he wouldn't have been drawn to me. In fact, I wouldn't have blamed him if he had run away from me, screaming!

> I doubt whether any healthy human being would have the fortitude to stick around with someone through extreme emotional sickness, particularly if that person has *never* been well, to wait for the final result—and at the same time remain well themselves. Love would be tainted with the infestation and decay of emotional illness.
>
> But somehow God transcends this. He sees us as we will be. He loves us as if we're already perfected. Through

that love, He gives us the grace and forgiveness we need to become the perfect people He loves.

JOURNAL ENTRY, JAN. 2, 2015

As I looked at the words in my journal that day, a question reverberated through my spirit: can we do any less? God's love for us results in His forgiveness. His forgiveness transforms us into loveable people. The spark igniting the transformation is love. We are left with a challenge the apostle John gave to early Christians. It resounds to those in our century too.

> "Beloved, if God so loved us, we also ought to love one another. If someone says, 'I love God,' and hates his brother, he is a liar; for the one who does not love his brother whom he has seen, cannot love God whom he has not seen."
>
> 1 JOHN 4:11, 20

12

BC and AD

For you were formerly darkness, but now you are Light in the Lord; walk as children of the Light.

Ephesians 5:8

When we've been hurt, sometimes we just want to curl up in a ball with our suffering. It's one thing to be wounded unintentionally or by someone with a mental illness. In some ways, those injuries are easier to forgive. We can understand the 'why' more easily; this helps us step out of our pain and into the other person's shoes.

But what about intentional, malevolent hurts? What about wrongs founded on others' pride and ambitions? What if we've been bruised by people who should have known better? Friends? Family? Christians we've opened our hearts to?

What about wounds so deep and treacherous that our worlds are rocked to their foundations? They shatter our dreams, our identities. They mean our lives will never be the same. What do we do when pure evil leaves only destruction and desolation in its path?

Sometimes we come to a turning point, when that next decision will determine the course of the rest of our lives. I've come across several of these. Most have come during painful seasons.

Make no mistake; when you or I encounter deep traumas, we often reach a crossroads. We have a choice to make between forgiveness, justice, vengeance, and reconciliation.

The Bible talks about all these concepts and recommends each action at one time or another. I'm sure all of us have heard preachers and politicians advocating for the various approaches. They are, in some ways, contradictory. How do we cut through the confusion to follow Jesus no matter where He leads?

The Bible is divided into two parts, as is human history: before and after Christ. That's because the world changed when Jesus entered it. Before Him, the only way for people to approach God was through a bloody and complex sacrificial system. After Him, coming to God became much simpler; now, children can often understand the kingdom of heaven better than adults.

Jesus' teachings turned the world upside down, stood 'common sense' on its head, and flushed out hypocrisy. So, followers of Jesus must always keep in mind His teachings and the world change they brought when looking to the Scriptures for guidance in how to live. He is the One who ties it all together—the old and the new covenant, the law and the prophets, the kingdom of God that is both coming and is now here.

We human beings repeatedly make mistakes in expressing ourselves. We sometimes have significant trouble communicating with one another. Misunderstandings are common. Humans struggle to interact with, and understand, other humans. How much more might we misread Someone who is not human! God recognizes this limitation.

> For My thoughts are not your thoughts,
> Nor are your ways My ways...
> For as the heavens are higher than the earth,
> So are My ways higher than your ways
> And My thoughts than your thoughts.
>
> ISAIAH 55:8–9

How can we possibly understand—and *not* misinterpret—God and His Word? The answer is Jesus. As the Son of God, He intimately knows the Father in a way we never can. Remember, He said, "No one knows the Son except the Father; nor does anyone know the Father except the Son, and anyone to whom the Son wills to reveal Him" (Matthew 11:27).

Jesus, His teachings, and His conduct on earth can help us learn what God wants of us, because only through Jesus is God the Father's perfect will revealed and completed.

So, what does this mean for our understanding of forgiveness, justice, vengeance, and reconciliation?

If Jesus recalibrated the whole Jewish religious system, then we would expect there to be variations in the application of key concepts between the Old and New Testaments. These differences would shed light on the impact Jesus makes in our lives when we're following and obeying Him. Let's do a brief word study of forgiveness, justice, vengeance, and reconciliation—comparing the Old and New Testaments—and focus on the questions below:

1. How many times does each testament mention these terms?
2. In what context are they mentioned?

Here, I will summarize the findings. If you want a little more detail, please see the Notes section at the end of this book.

Forgive/forgiven/forgiveness
Old Testament—57 mentions
New Testament—75 mentions

The New Testament refers to forgiveness much more than the Old Testament does—especially when we consider the Old Testament is more than three times longer than the New Testament. The concept of forgiveness was by no means foreign to the previous authors. There are, however, subtle differences in tone.

Old Testament writers tend to request God's forgiveness for themselves or for someone else. They describe a complex sacrificial system set up to win favour from God.[1]

By contrast, New Testament writers adopt a brighter mood. Jesus and His followers travelled around proclaiming God's redemption and forgiveness to all who repented and believed. The New Testament says outright that there is no longer a need for sin offerings when forgiveness is given. People living in those times solicited pardon from God and each other. The Scriptures are peppered with exhortations for Jesus' followers to forgive. Of course, Jesus also provided us with abundant examples of His own forgiveness towards humankind.[2]

Justice

Old Testament—125 mentions
New Testament—11 mentions

The difference between the Old and New Testaments for the word 'justice' is dramatic.

God's people sometimes pleaded for justice in Old Testament times. The king was its dispenser, and Jehovah was described as the God of justice. The wicked despised it, but God commanded His people to never pervert it.

The New Testament refers to God as the keeper of justice. In a few cases, Jesus decried the Pharisees' lack of impartiality.

Avenge/revenge/vengeance

Old Testament—90 mentions
New Testament—10 mentions

Again, the Old and New Testaments differ widely in their use of 'vengeance' and its variants.

In the Old Testament, the righteous rejoiced when they saw God take vengeance upon their enemies. God's people looked with anticipation to the future 'day of the Lord' or 'day of vengeance' against those who had oppressed them. Sometimes the people of Israel evened the score; at others, they asked God to get even for them.[3]

In the New Testament, all but two instances refer to God as the avenger while we are not. For example, God said, "Vengeance is mine, I will repay" (Romans 12:19). The Bible never indicates that Christians retaliated against their enemies.[4]

Reconcile/reconciliation
Old Testament—1 mention
New Testament—15 mentions

Old Testament writers didn't discuss reconciliation in a personal or relational manner. They talked about trying to reconcile actions with beliefs.

Meanwhile, *all* instances of reconciliation in the New Testament are between us and God or us and other Christians. We are meant to be active in restoring harmony; God or we are the initiators in these scenarios. We don't passively wait for our spiritual siblings to start the process.

The conclusion from this study is clear: the application of forgiveness differs drastically before and after Jesus. We are to be a people not of vengeance but of reconciliation. We are to be people who would rather suffer injustice than allow a spirit of unforgiveness to fester in our hearts.

We are to live like our Saviour—in humility, without clinging to human ideas of 'rights'. Jesus wants us to be living sacrifices; when we lay down our selves, we will be transformed into Spirit-enabled, flesh and blood vessels through whom God can work miraculous deeds and draw many to Himself.

Closing Part III
Food for Thought

I ONCE DID A WEB SEARCH ON the word 'forgiveness'. One of the first results described it as a "matter of life or death for Christians".[1] I initially recoiled from the melodrama of this statement. After a few minutes, though, I realized it was true. We reap what we sow. If we refuse to forgive others, God will not forgive us.

Ancient versions of justice required retribution. But we don't live in Old Testament times. If we want to have access to New Testament grace and salvation, we cannot revert to the old ways of vengeance when it suits us. We have to choose.

As a prison inmate who converted to Christianity once wrote, "The blood of Abel cryed vengeance, the blood of Jesus cryed mercy."[2]

When we refuse to forgive others, this demonstrates pride. Jesus sacrificed His life on the cross to offer forgiveness to all people, including those who have hurt us. We are essentially saying the other party's wrongdoing is much more serious than any evil we might have committed—and thus is unforgivable.

When we refuse to forgive, we also set ourselves above God. Our standards are higher than His. He may forgive, but we will not. The sin is too grievous. The wound is too deep.

Dare we place ourselves in this position? Dare we usurp the authority over forgiveness that is God's alone?

These are uncomfortable truths. They're inconvenient. Scary. We may be tempted to avoid them. Yet, if my house is ablaze, and I choose to go on with my life as though nothing is wrong, I place myself in great danger.

If we ignore the things that scare us, we may end up in greater trouble. Let us not turn a blind eye to Jesus' teachings. Let's dig deep and take hold of them—because when we embrace them, we also embrace freedom.

Going Deeper

1. Why is love our most important Christian characteristic?

2. When has there been a disconnect between what you say you believe and what you do? Confess these things before Jesus and ask Him to empower you to align your words with your deeds.

3. Is there anyone you need to forgive right now?

4. God's love for us results in His forgiveness, which transforms us into loveable people. That transformation all starts with love. How can you show this same tenderness to others? Write down your ideas.

5. "If your brother or sister sins against you, rebuke them; and if they repent, forgive them. Even if they sin against you seven times in a day and seven times come back to you saying, 'I repent', you must forgive them." (Luke 17:3–4, NIV)

   How do you feel when you read these words?

Part IV

Freedom in Forgiveness

EACH CULTURE CONTRIBUTES ITS OWN unique perspective to the human mosaic of understanding who God is and how He interacts with His children. This lends richness to the worldwide church.

In North America, we tend to focus on our salvation as a gift from God, a result of His loving Fatherhood. The church in Africa seems to understand hospitality and caring for one another's needs to a much deeper degree than in the West.[1] The church in Japan has its own distinctive contribution.

Japan is a country replete with disaster—both natural and man-made. One has barely finished, the people have only begun to pick up the pieces, when the next one comes to knock everything down again.

Historically, Japanese Christians have suffered greatly for their faith. Starting in the late sixteenth century, the Japanese government began a campaign to stamp out Christianity, going so far as to crucify Christians in Nagasaki.[2] So, Japanese Christians place a high value on perseverance through difficulty. They tend to focus on Jesus as the One who suffers along with us.

This is something I've always loved and appreciated about our God. He is not ignorant of our suffering. He can sympathize with us and our weaknesses. He won't ask anything of us that He has not first done Himself.

Talk about relief—knowing that no matter what we encounter, there will always be Someone by our side who intimately understands! Hard circumstances give us extraordinary opportunities for intimacy with our heavenly Father.

Yet, He does not want us to remain in pain and suffering indefinitely. His plans for us are much better than that. He wants to help us walk the difficult road from betrayal and hurt to forgiveness, love, and freedom. We can find clues on how to do this by looking at how God forgives us.

13

How God Forgives Us

> *Whoever said revenge is sweet never tasted the sweetness of forgiveness.*
>
> MARC CHERNOFF, AUTHOR AND BLOGGER

THIS PASSAGE ALWAYS TOUCHES ME with its tenderness:

> For as high as the heavens are above the earth,
> So great is His lovingkindness toward those who fear Him.
> As far as the east is from the west,
> So far has He removed our transgressions from us.
>
> PSALM 103:11–12

These verses remind me of a parent and child. The parent says, "How much do you love me?"

Stretching out his arms as wide as they can go, the child exclaims, "This much!"

In this case, it's God who's widening His arms—and they are very big indeed! He isn't afraid of being undignified.

"How much do You love me?"

"This much." His arms get really tall.

"How much have You forgiven me?"

"This much!" He stretches as far as the east is from the west.

God is extravagant that way.

The apostle Peter once asked Jesus an important question: "How many times should I forgive? Seven times?"

Jesus replied, "Seventy times seven" (Matthew 18:21–22).

Four hundred and ninety times. That doesn't seem so outrageous. I would have been more comfortable if Jesus had said, "One million times"; I'm sure I'll sin against my husband and family more than four hundred and ninety times during my life.

But Jesus combined His godly extravagance with gentleness toward human frailty. We tend to get overwhelmed. We turn off and tune out the impossible. Jesus took Peter's number—the highest he was willing to go—and multiplied it by another, ten times bigger. Though large, it wasn't so inconceivable that Peter would give up.

I have a feeling that if Peter's original number had been one million, then Jesus would have said, "10,000,000 × 1,000,000 times".

Jesus is like that. He's patient with our limitedness. He knows our smallness and comes to meet and teach us right where we are.

We see this again in another set of verses, dear to my heart:

> The steps of a man are established by the Lord,
> And He delights in his way.

> When he falls, he will not be hurled headlong,
> Because the Lord is the One who holds his hand.
>
> PSALM 37:23–24

In reading this passage, I've always had the image of a toddler and her father in my mind's eye. She's wobbling along with halting steps, and the father is patiently walking alongside, holding her hand to steady and protect her from harm.

When first learning these verses in university, I mis-memorized a word. I thought the Bible said, "if he falls". What tremendous release and freedom were mine when I realized the wording was not *if* but *when*. Our Father is tender and patient and understands our weakness. He knows we *will* fall. There is no question about it. But He will be present to catch us and to help us regain our footing.

God extravagantly meets us in our human frailty. Yet, as Jesus' teaching shows, there is no limit to the forgiveness we should offer others, because there's no limit to the forgiveness He offers us.

If there were a cap on forgiveness, there would also be a cap on freedom. We would constantly be on a countdown of how many 'chances' we had left.

I well remember a time when I thought such a countdown was real. Whenever I sinned, I was afraid of God. I knew I had done something wrong but was hesitant to confess it to Him. I tried to hide my wrongdoing and pretend it didn't exist.

Then one day I heard a song by Andrew Peterson:

> All of my life I've held on to this fear
> These thistles and vines ensnare and entwine
> What flowers appear
> It's the fear that I'll fall one too many times
> It's the fear that His love is no better than mine
> But He tells me that
>
> Just as I am and just as I was
> Just as I will be He loves me, He does
> He showed me the day that
> He shed His own blood
> He loves me, oh, He loves me, He does[1]

Now and then we undergo a cosmic shift in our spiritual understanding. This first happens when we come to understand and accept Jesus' sacrifice for us. Later, we may come to recognize something about God, some exquisite characteristic or bedrock truth, different from anything we've known before. When I heard Andrew Peterson's song, I experienced one of those moments. My understanding shifted.

> It's the fear that I'll fall one too many times
> It's the fear that His love is no better than mine[2]

Those words echoed in my brain. How many of us walk around in fear of this very thing! At times, we translate our anxiety into attempts to hide our sins and temptations from

God. We don't talk with Him about them. Perhaps He will reject us if He knows. As author and public speaker Brennan Manning put it, "Sometimes we harbour an unexpressed suspicion that he cannot handle all that goes on in our minds and hearts. We doubt that he can accept our hateful thoughts, cruel fantasies, and bizarre dreams. We wonder how he would deal with our primitive urges, our inflated illusions, and our exotic mental castles. The deep resistance to making ourselves so vulnerable, so naked, so totally unprotected is our implicit way of saying, 'Jesus, I trust you, but there are limits.'"[3]

Sometimes we allow our disgrace to become bigger than our God. We think that by not confessing our sins to Him, we can retain a bit of our dignity. Like Adam and Eve in the garden of Eden, we hide ourselves away.

But the truth is, He already knows. The truth is, we are *retaining* our shame by hiding it. Beth Moore was so right in declaring, "God never abuses His authority. He also never shames. Do you remember the woman at the well? After her encounter with Jesus, she ran into town saying, 'He told me everything I ever did!' (John 4:39) And she wasn't ashamed! Do you know why? Because when Christ takes authority over our pasts, and we allow Him to confront them, treat them, and heal them, we exchange our shame for dignity!"[4]

When we try to sneak around our Saviour, we do nothing but cripple our own resistance to temptation. One thing is certain—we "may conceal our infirmity, even from our dearest friend, but we will not conceal it from our worst enemy."[5] Satan knows exactly when and where we have given in.

Our spiritual adversary will do anything—anything!—to exploit our weaknesses and unresolved transgressions. Make no mistake: two beings know about the wrongdoing we've confessed to no one—God, our Father; and Satan, our enemy. When we don't confess our sins to God, we show we trust His forgiveness *less* than we trust Satan.

14
Selling Our Birthright

God didn't give us the strength to get back on our feet so that we can run back to the same thing that knocked us down.

Marvin Sapp, pastor and singer-songwriter

My sister, Julia, used to smoke as a way of coping with stress.

My mother was a melodramatic person. She had specific ideas about acceptable Christian behaviour, and smoking was on the 'unacceptable' list.

On the night before Peter's and my wedding, Julia sneaked out for some stress release by the side of the house. She'd sporadically encountered one of our neighbours there, feeding her own craving.

"Don't tell my parents," the neighbour had pleaded.

Her companion wasn't there that night; Julia was alone with her cigarette. The evening was warm. Our windows were open, and the smoke wafted in.

My sister had told Mum she'd stopped smoking months before, but the smell carried its own declaration to our noses. Eyes hardened, lips tightened, out Mum stomped to discover her wayward daughter. I still remember the voice-cracking passion floating up on the warm fall air: "You've been saved from this! Why would you return to this addiction? You've been saved to be free!"

That cry reverberates in my mind today as I consider how often we abandon our freedom in Christ for shackles of slavery. Bitterness and unforgiveness are two of the strongest chains we choose.

When we find ourselves imprisoned once more, do we try to escape by entering into godly lament and repentance? Or do we shrug, accept the new status quo, and start decorating our jail cells?

Jesus paid dearly to release us from slavery, death, and sin. Yet too often, we follow in Esau's footsteps, exchanging our birthrights for bowls of stew. Instead of cherishing our freedom, we throw it on the discard pile. It's like bringing a precious, priceless gift to a pawn shop and trading it for pocket change.

Sin, too, can be an addiction. King Solomon once said a fool returning to his folly is like a dog circling back to its vomit. Each of us struggles with the temptation to come back to the vomit of sin, decay, and death. At times, we scoop it into our mouths, re-chew, and call it a feast.

Can you hear the passionate, gut-wrenching cry of the Holy Spirit?

"For what have you been freed? You've been saved from this! Why would you return to this addiction?"

How cheaply we sell our freedom.

This reminds me of the parable of the unforgiving servant in Matthew 18. He owed his master a great debt. When he and his family were about to be sold into slavery to recoup the loss, he begged for more time. The master took pity on the man and forgave the entire amount.

The forgiven servant then went out and found another man who owed him a fraction of his own former debt. He incarcerated the other fellow until the loan was repaid.

When the master heard of this, he was outraged and sent his underling to prison.

Why was the master so angry? Had the servant cooked the books? Had he stolen the silverware on the way out? This anger was severe enough for the master to imprison a man for whom he had felt compassion not long before.

Jesus tells us why the master was outraged—the servant didn't pass on the clemency he had accepted.

We, too, are obligated to extend to others the mercy we've received from God. Such mercy looks like forgiveness. Without *receiving* our heavenly Father's forgiveness, we can't have a restored relationship with Him. Without *giving* forgiveness, we lose everything that defines us as Christians. In essence, forgiven people forgive people—or they should! If we don't forgive others, we can't expect our Father in heaven to forgive us.

Sometimes a disconnect forms between our outward and inward realities. This was the case when the unforgiving servant was, well, unforgiving. Outwardly, he was free; inwardly,

Selling Our Birthright

he was imprisoned by his own sinful, unmerciful attitudes. He might have continued in this inner prison indefinitely. In a way, it was a mercy the master jailed him.

Now and then mercy does something that seems harsh to highlight a worse internal reality. When a child requires correction, this may appear unkind in the moment, but consequences help teach him his actions are wrong. The discipline helps shape the child's character and future. Likewise, the master's punishment shone a spotlight on his servant's internal reality and gave him a chance to repent and change. Perhaps, in time, the servant would have realized that timeless truth: "Forgiveness is unlocking the door to set someone free and realizing that you were the prisoner!"[1]

April 20, 1999, was a day that changed everything in the way American students, teachers, and parents experienced school, both at the time and for generations to come. Late that Tuesday morning, several pupils were studying in the library of Columbine High School, in Littleton, Colorado, when a teacher ran in, shouting for everyone to get under the tables. Gunshots sounded in the hallway.

Two armed teenagers entered the library, giddy and happy, as if playing a video game, as they mowed down their fellow students.

They saw a girl named Cassie under a table, praying.

"Do you believe in God?" one asked.

Cassie paused. "Yes."

They shot her.

The two boys were senior students at that school. After their rampage, they committed suicide.

Cassie's story reverberated throughout the Christian community around the world. A martyrdom on American soil was almost beyond belief. Cassie and her courage were standards to follow. She had been willing to give up her life rather than deny her faith.

Her family faced the challenges of how to cope with the tragedy and how to deal with their loss and anger in the face of such destruction. They decided to forgive. The words of Misty Bernall, Cassie's mother, still ring with truth: "Anger is a destructive emotion. It eats away at whatever peace you have, and in the end it causes nothing but greater pain than you began with."

Jesus longs to free us from the painful burden of unforgiveness. He wants to construct a better future for us, but He won't force us into anything. So, now we must decide what we want.[2]

15
Willing Victims?

The word 'forgive' is one of the most powerful words in the Bible. A healthy life, spiritually and psychologically, is impossible without forgiveness.

EUGENE CARPENTER AND PHILIP COMFORT,
HOLMAN TREASURY OF KEY BIBLE WORDS

WHEN YOU OR I HAVE been wounded, sometimes pain stretches on and on with no end in sight. We may resent the people who have hurt us. We may hate that their actions have changed us. Our inner self-portraits undergo a radical transformation. We're no longer our old selves. The label 'victim' is plastered on our spirits. We can't seem to escape the wrongs we've suffered.

In talking with friends and even people we barely know, our painful stories flow out. Soon others see us as victims, because that's the way we see ourselves.

When something brushes up against our wounds, we lash out.

It's okay, we tell ourselves. *It's just because I'm in pain. It's because I'm a victim.*

We may gossip about the person who hurt us.

These people need to know what she did to me. They need to know what I've gone through.

In trying to look after our injured selves, we may behave in ways we wouldn't have condoned before.

It's okay. I need to take care of myself. I'm a victim.

Immediately after our bodies are physically wounded, they can go into shock. The same is true for our spiritual and emotional selves. We need time to emerge from stupor before forming coherent thoughts and opinions about what has happened. Only then can we process our feelings and approach forgiveness from a place of authenticity.

Eventually, we will have to forgive. Even if we're still in shock, acknowledging this necessity will make the journey a little less arduous. It's not healthy to wilfully remain in shock so we have an excuse for not forgiving. We should beware of cultivating a victim mentality because it's often not temporary. This attitude can take over and become a lifelong addiction.

A victim mindset feels safe. It's something we know. It's gotten us through tough, painful times. Yet when we embrace it, our entire identity becomes wrapped up in victimhood. I've been there. I've found it scary to go out, alone, into the world, without a companion. Victimhood fills that role. We can blame it for bad decisions and wrong attitudes rather than taking responsibility for our own thoughts and deeds.

We turn into *willing* sufferers. When that happens, the truth becomes uglier than we realize. We are now victimizing *ourselves*.

Some of the most wicked people in history were at one time victims:

Person	Childhood	Adulthood
Joseph Stalin	• Father was an alcoholic who beat him,[1] his siblings, and his mother[2] • Had moved nine times by the age of 10[3]	Stalin would rule the Soviet Union for thirty years, instituting labour camps, creating famines, torturing people, and engaging in mass murder. Not including deaths in World War II, he would be responsible for the deaths of more than 20 million people.
Adolf Hitler	• Younger brother died when Adolf was 3 years old[4] • Suffered child abuse[5] • Took care of his mother; she died of cancer when he was 18[6]	Hitler and those who followed him murdered tens of millions of people—Jews, Christians, and others he considered inferior.
Ivan the Terrible	• Father died when Ivan was 3[7] • Mother died when Ivan was 8[8] • Was neglected[9]	Ivan began torturing animals and injuring old men and women in his childhood.[10] During his reign as tsar of Russia, he would kill tens of thousands of people[11] "with calculated and symbolic cruelty", and even murder his only healthy heir.[12]

These are considered some of the most evil men in history. Their victimhood turned to self-pity and entitlement.

Never underestimate the power of self-pity. It is insidious. If it's strong enough, we can use it to justify any atrocity. It deceives us into thinking we don't have to forgive. It focuses us on the misdeeds of others so we can ignore our own.

When I was a little girl, my mother used to tell this story:

> Imagine you're walking in a snowy field. You're bundled up, but—brr!—it's cold outside! You want to warm up with a cup of hot chocolate, wrap your chilled fingers around that toasty mug, and hear the crackle of a fireplace as it melts your frozen toes.
>
> There's a coffee shop to your right, but a fence is in the way. The entire field is enclosed. To exit, you have to walk straight ahead to a gate. You start towards it but soon gaze to your right, enticed by the promise of things to come. A few minutes later, your eyes return to the gate.
>
> In what direction will your footsteps be heading?
>
> I can almost guarantee you will have veered off course. Your steps will have turned to the right—towards the coffee shop.
>
> We always tend to walk in the direction our eyes are looking. This is just as true in the emotional and spiritual realms as it is in the physical one.

An unforgiving spirit gives birth to an emotional baby—bitterness. It rehashes wrongs and rehearses revenge. Little do we realize that we imitate the people we think about most.

Do we want that? Do we want to become victimizers ourselves, possibly of people we love? This is not the glorious destiny Jesus died to give us. To embrace Jesus' plan, we must be willing to shed the safety of our victimhood and take those risky-feeling steps towards freedom.

It's no wonder the apostle Paul exhorts us to set our minds on "whatever is true, whatever is honorable, whatever is right, whatever is pure, whatever is lovely, whatever is of good repute" (Philippians 4:8). We are to concentrate on things that are excellent and worthy of praise because *we* want to be people of excellence, worthy of praise.

When we adjust the direction of our gaze and focus on the forgiveness of the cross rather than on the hurt that's pierced our hearts, our futures are infused with Jesus' hope and promise. He died to set us free from the bondage of bitterness. He freed us to be victors, not victims. He calls us to become healthy, whole people.

We're left with a decision. We may not have had a choice over what happened to us, but we have a choice *now*. It is a sacred gift God has given us.

Here are our options:

- Will we choose to remain casualties of others' malice forever and allow our identities to be defined by their deeds?

- Or will we acknowledge the evil but not permit it to define us?

- Will we trade in our freedom for bondage to pain and self-pity?
- Or will we courageously step into the victory Jesus purchased for us on Calvary?
- Will we allow our entire existence to be defined by an ugly season?
- Or will we embrace the glorious future Jesus has planned for us?

May our addiction be to Jesus rather than to our victimhood!

We may not have the strength or ability to take those first steps towards forgiveness on our own. But we can allow Jesus' Spirit, who is already strong, to obey through us. As Galatians 2:20 says, "I have been crucified with Christ; and it is no longer I who live, but Christ lives in me." This is not an abdication of our responsibility to obey but an acknowledgement of our weakness and complete dependence on Him.

In reaching out for Him, we may realize we've been in His arms all along. God can redeem and heal lives filled with abuse. He can "give back the years the locusts have eaten" (Joel 2:25, my paraphrase) if only we have the courage to let Him perform His divine surgery on our hearts.

Make no mistake—if we are deciding whether or not to forgive, we are standing at a crossroads. Our decisions today can have huge repercussions that will echo through time and eternity—for good or for evil. The choice is ours.

Closing Part IV

Food for Thought

HASHIM GARRET WAS A FIFTEEN-year-old teenager wandering the streets with a Brooklyn gang, oblivious to his mother's warnings. Trying to prove he was tough, he would do anything the other gang members asked of him. When told to beat someone up, he would. When told to shoot someone, he did. Eventually, though, he stopped wanting to do everything the others asked of him.[1]

One day on a walk to the corner store, Hashim was shot six times by another kid with a gun. He would later learn his friends had gotten impatient with him. If he wasn't willing to do whatever they said, he was a liability. They'd decided killing him would be the easiest way to solve their problem.

Hashim lay bleeding on the sidewalk. "God, please don't let me die," he prayed. At once, his fear evaporated. People came by to help, and he was taken to a hospital.

Paralyzed below the waist, Hashim now had a radically different life. He needed help going to the bathroom and was consumed with rage and a desire for revenge. His emotional and physical pain were intense and unending.

As he lay in his hospital bed one day, the thought came to him that he should forgive. That conviction grew, and he followed it.

Now he's a consultant and motivational speaker who travels to schools around the United States. He calls the day he was shot "one of the best days of my life, because it helped me to see things clearly, and gave me a new lease on life."[2]

How could this transformation have happened? In Hashim's words, "If you have forgiveness in your heart, bad things may still happen, but a bad thing can be a blessing in disguise."[3]

Going Deeper

1. Describe a time when you tried to hide your sin from God. What happened? How did it affect your spiritual life?

2. Read the following verses.

   > The steps of a man are established by the Lord,
   > And He delights in his way.
   > When he falls, he will not be hurled headlong,
   > Because the Lord is the One who holds his hand.
   >
   > Psalm 37:23–24

How do they make you feel? How might they change your outlook on life?

3. How may an addiction to a victim mentality rob us of the glorious destiny God has in store for us?

4. Try a meditation exercise. Close your eyes. Slowly become aware of your body. Notice how it feels—whether the muscles are tight or loose, tired, heavy, energetic, painful. Now, how does your body react to the following statement?

"I am a victor, not a victim."

Pay special attention to sensations in your chest, stomach, throat, and muscles. These will give you clues about your initial emotions when approaching this idea. Continue to meditate and pray, allowing the truth to sink into your spirit.

Part V

How to Forgive

WE'VE BEEN LAYING THE FOUNDATION for what comes next. Forgiveness is such a difficult task that we need to know beforehand what it is, why we're doing it, and what the benefits are. Without a clear understanding of these things, our resolve to carry it out will likely fail.

Let's now move on to examine attitudes that can affect our success. Then, we'll discuss how to generate forgiveness within our own hearts and actions.

16

Shaping our Attitudes

I beseech you to think it possible you may be mistaken.

OLIVER CROMWELL, IN A LETTER TO THE
GENERAL ASSEMBLY OF THE CHURCH OF SCOTLAND

HUMAN BEINGS MELD PHYSICAL, emotional, psychological, and spiritual realities into a single, complex existence. We're constantly processing so much information that sometimes we make assumptions without realizing it.

In one study, researchers Christopher Chabris and Daniel Simons arranged for two basketball teams—one wearing white and one wearing black—to run around a court, passing balls. They instructed observers to ignore the actions of the black side and count when players on the white side passed to each other. This was an intensive psychological task, requiring a great deal of concentration.

A woman dressed in a gorilla suit stepped onto the court partway through the experiment, thumped her chest, and walked off. She was visible for approximately nine seconds.

After the exercise was complete, observers were asked if they had noticed anything unusual. Many were stumped.

Thousands of people have seen the video of this experiment but, after viewing it once, about half of them don't remember the gorilla and are *sure* it was never there. They can't seem to come to grips with missing such a significant event. They often have to watch the recording again, without counting, before they can acknowledge the gorilla's presence.

This study has profound psychological ramifications. When we're distracted by important tasks, we can be blind to other events. Our concentration becomes so focussed on the important that we miss the remarkable. This experiment offers a second conclusion: not only can we miss what is obvious, but also we can be "blind to our own blindness."[1]

Perceptions shape experience. It's difficult to accept that our reality is not objective but is shaped by many subjective factors. We tend to assume all mentally healthy people experience the same things when placed in the same situations. This is not the case. As the gorilla experiment shows, focus can have significant impact on perception and observation.

We're apt to take thoughts and intentions into account when examining our own conduct. At times, rather than focussing on the outside world, we get preoccupied by our inner lives. Our brains are so full we fail to realize it when action doesn't align with intent.

Sometimes other people can see this better than we can, because they aren't distracted by the activity in our minds. They only observe our behaviours and the results. It is perhaps for this reason Nobel prize winning psychologist Daniel Kahneman said, "It is easier to recognize other people's mistakes than our own."

Lest we take this observation as a license to be critical of others' conduct, we should also remember we tend to *attribute* thoughts and intentions to other people based on their behaviours and our own biases. This comes with its own set of risks.

Many of us like to analyze other people from a psychological standpoint. This practice is prone to error because we don't know everything about the people we're observing. Our assumptions could be—and often are—wrong. Each person's thought patterns, logic, and previous experiences vary. There's no way we can know what's going on in their heads. Even when they summarize their thoughts, there's much more under the surface that we cannot guess.

Through the character Fetyukovitch in *The Brothers Karamazov*, Fyodor Dostoyevsky warns, "There are things which are even worse, even more fatal than the most malicious and consciously unfair attitude. It is worse if we are carried away by the artistic instinct, by the desire to create, so to speak, a romance, especially if God has endowed us with psychological insight. Psychology lures even most serious people into romancing, and quite unconsciously. I am speaking of the abuse of psychology."[2]

When we create other people's supposed psychologies without allowing them to correct errors in our pet theories, we risk manufacturing fictitious caricatures that bear them only a passing resemblance. This type of psychology can be devastating.

Equally destructive is the analysis we may apply to ourselves. We may think that if we're sincere, if we have clear consciences, then we must be in the right. When we adopt this mindset, we are in perilous mental and moral territory. Sincerity does not define truth. If it did, then should I come back from Japan and in all sincerity make the mistake of driving on the left-hand side of the road, neither I nor any of the drivers in oncoming traffic would be harmed.

We can earnestly believe in something and be earnestly wrong. As we navigate conflict's perilous terrain, let us not forget a vital truth:

> Our consciences are not objective measures of wrongdoing. They are entirely subjective.

Conscience is only an indicator of the sin we *recognize*. We may be oblivious to other misdeeds through fear, pride, wilful blindness, or a habit of ignoring our own moral principles. It is possible to harden our hearts and sear our consciences[3] so they are no longer sensitive to intentional evil.

The wise are wary of claiming a clear conscience. More often than not, when those words pass our lips, we ought to run to God in repentance—of pride at the minimum and perhaps of other sins.

The apostle Paul recognized the duality that exists between a clear conscience and actual wrongdoing. He said,

"My conscience is clear, but that does not make me innocent. It is the Lord who judges me." (1 Corinthians 4:4, NIV)

If it's possible to be guilty even with a clear conscience, then conscience must not have the final say on sinfulness. We can be sinful without realizing it. A clear conscience only means we don't *perceive* any wrongdoing. It doesn't mean none has taken place.

King David recognized this dichotomy.

> Who can discern their own errors?
> Forgive my hidden faults.
> Keep your servant also from willful sins;
> may they not rule over me.
> Then I will be blameless,
> innocent of great transgression.
>
> PSALM 19:12–13, NIV

He identified two types of sin[4] in these verses:

1. WILFUL SINS

These are what usually come to mind when we consider sins; we are aware of having committed them. They stem from rebellion. We want our own way and are willing to ignore God to get it.

2. HIDDEN FAULTS

We cannot identify our own hidden faults. In fact, when David uses the term 'error' in Psalm 19, the original word is *shagah*, which in Hebrew means "sin through ignorance".[5] As Beth Moore says, "Rebellion is not the only way to get into trouble." Ignorance can be just as deadly. Only when we're cleansed from both kinds of sin can we be considered blameless and innocent.

The prophet Malachi provided a valuable case study. He wrote to a people who thought they were honouring and serving God, when they were doing the opposite. When God rebuked them, they kept asking, "How have we dishonoured You? How have we disobeyed You?" (Malachi 1:6–8, 2:17, 3:13–14)

By all appearances, the people were sincere. They were so blinded by their own arrogance and disobedience that they couldn't tell the difference between righteousness and wickedness. Their consciences were so jaded they thought they were clear.

Chapter 3 ends with God looking to the future and speaking to His people. "So you will again distinguish between the righteous and the wicked, between one who serves God and one who does not serve Him." (Malachi 3:18)

This implies that the people could *not* distinguish between the righteous and the wicked. They could *not* tell who was serving God and who was not. Their spiritual compasses were so broken they thought north was south and south was north. Yet they, too, could have claimed clear consciences.

In Acts 5, the apostles were called to the temple to give testimony before the Sanhedrin, a tribunal of rabbis. Peter told these religious leaders about Jesus' true identity as Prince and Saviour, the One whom God exalted to His right hand in heaven. The Sanhedrin reacted with murderous rage. However, Gamaliel, a widely respected leader, counselled the others to wait them out. If the apostles' cause was not of God, it would fade away now that Jesus wasn't around. Only divine intervention could prevent the Jesus movement from collapsing. If it continued and the Sanhedrin had done nothing, they wouldn't have inadvertently fought against God. In the end, the council followed this recommendation.

The most interesting thing about this passage is the Sanhedrin took Gamaliel's advice. This implies they did not *want* to fight God.

They didn't want to oppose God, yet they killed Jesus. Why? There are a few possibilities that can resolve the dissonance.

1. The Sanhedrin didn't believe God sent Jesus.

2. At first they believed God sent Jesus, but later they thought Jesus became ambitious and power-hungry, undermining their authority. The prophet run amok had to be stopped.

3. They didn't consider a heavenly point of view when they decided their plan of action. They were blinded by their own fear that the Romans would remove them

from their homeland. When Gamaliel outlined their options, the council (of course) chose the one that meant they wouldn't be fighting against God.

How important it is to submit every decision—even the 'obvious' ones—to our heavenly Father! How easily we may choose solutions that mean we fight against Him and commit atrocities that are the opposite of our intentions.

It's vital to recognize that we see only a portion of our own sinfulness. Humility is born when we realize the fallibility of our consciences. Then, we begin to pray holy prayers like this one:

> "God, I don't want to be jaded so that all I can see is my own version of right. I can pervert truth. I'm a sinful human. I don't have a corner on righteousness, and I never will. Please search my heart and see if there is any wicked way in me. Cut it out from me today, Lord! Let me be pure and holy in Your sight."

We are guaranteed to be wrong in something. It's not a matter of saying we *could* be wrong. We are *certainly* wrong. We just don't know where our errors are yet.

> We don't know how we are wrong, and
> we don't know how wrong we are.

Shaping our Attitudes

We can do nothing to change the fact that we are finite, sinful beings. Cognitive biases and limitations in our attention won't disappear anytime soon. Be that as it may, we *can* adopt attitudes of humility. We will never have the edge on what is right and wrong.

How important it is to submit ourselves, our thoughts, and our actions to God for His examination, reproof, and correction. Only then are we able to live lives holy and pleasing to Him. We're like babies sitting in a bathtub, needing their Father to bathe them. We don't know all the places that are dirty. We don't even fully understand the concept of dirt and can by no means cleanse ourselves. We have neither the skill nor the cleanliness. Only something clean can wash away the grime from something grubby. So, we come to our Father, sit in our tub, and ask Him to bathe us, scrub us clean, and impart His freshness and life to our souls once more.

Humility is key when we consider sin and holiness. Without it, we are unlikely to emerge from times of hurt without committing sins ourselves—against those who have wounded us, against God, and perhaps against innocent people. Rather than perpetuating the pain that has scarred us, we can be instruments of healing. God can redeem even our injuries for good.

Jesus once said, "Why do you look at the speck that is in your brother's eye, but do not notice the log that is in your own eye? Or how can you say to your brother, 'Brother, let me take out the speck that is in your eye,' when you yourself do not see the log that is in your own eye? You hypocrite, first take the log out of your own eye, and then you will see clearly to take out the speck that is in your brother's eye." (Luke 6:41–42)

When we become critical, we disable ourselves from growing spiritually. We impair our capacity to absorb and apply godly correction. We so focus on pointing out the faults in others that we lose the ability to scrutinize our own lives in humility.

No wonder Jesus said, "Judge not, lest you be judged" (Matthew 7:1, BLB). When He said this, I don't think He meant God judges us tit for tat. He is not reading through our lives, circling those times we criticized others in red pen, and then saying, "Okay, Valerie judged someone. Now it's time for Me to judge her."

It's all a matter of focus. When we criticize others, our ability to examine ourselves begins to slip. We become more and more sinful without even realizing it. We harden our hearts towards the conviction of the Holy Spirit and render ourselves unteachable. That's what leads God to judge us.

The Russian writer Aleksandr Solzhenitsyn once said, "The line dividing good and evil cuts through the heart of every human being." The apostle Paul said something similar: "All have sinned and fall short of the glory of God" (Romans 3:23). It's vital to acknowledge and embrace this teaching. We all have sinful hearts. There is no exception.

If we are wise, we remember that judging other people is a waste of energy, especially when there's so much to condemn about our own behaviour. This awareness creates an attitude foundational to our capacity for offering forgiveness. In acknowledging our own sins, we recognize our conduct in the misdeeds of others. We become aware of our own corrupt tendencies and are able to say, "There, but for the grace of God, go I." We grow into people who treat those broken by sin with gentleness, compassion, and understanding.

The mercy we show flows from the mercy we receive from God. In fact, when we forgive others, we "demonstrate that we have been forgiven. So the telling line is this: If we refuse to be merciful, there is only one reason—we have never understood the grace of Christ."[6]

When we have compassion on those who have wronged us, our torment declines. We don't rehash the things that have happened to us; those jagged, painful edges begin to wear away. In time, we forget their sharpness.

The phrase 'forgive and forget' should never apply to the person who receives forgiveness. If we're in the wrong, we do well to bear in mind the extraordinary pardon we've been granted.[7]

On the other half of the equation, we who forgive have a unique opportunity to grow in our understanding of God's gift to us. We glimpse a sliver of what His forgiveness cost Him. Exhibiting mercy towards others has a powerful capacity to feed our gratitude to God.

17

Forgiveness in Practice

> *Little children, let us not love with word or with tongue,*
> *but in deed and truth.*
>
> 1 JOHN 3:18

MEMORY AND FORGIVENESS HAVE SIGNIFICANT neurochemical effects on the brain. If we choose not to forgive, we tend to rehash the hurt. Our memories are stored in specific physical structures in our minds, so when we replay them, it becomes easier and easier to recall the details.[1]

It's like walking through a patch of tall grass. The more I take the same path, the more the foliage gets folded back and worn away. Soon, it's no trouble to walk that path because my feet can find purchase more easily on the dirt underneath than on the grass itself.

This happens when we memorize information for a test in school, and it also happens when we replay memories of traumatic events. We are essentially memorizing the trauma.[2]

We have a choice. As teacher and author Terry C. Muck puts it, "We can either review that memory, rehearsing it into a vividly enhanced mental image, or we can choose not to allow its repetition, thereby relegating it to the unconscious. That mental, neurochemical choice is called forgiveness. The memory is still there, but when life stimuli bring it to mind, we choose to extinguish it rather than reinforce it."[3]

When we do this, we are following the apostle Paul's admonition to take our thoughts captive and submit them to our Lord Jesus Christ. We don't have to be slaves to our thoughts. They should serve us. What great freedom lies in this realization!

The idea of taking our thoughts captive can sound daunting if you've never done it before. To begin with, it's important to pray. The first time you attempt this form of submission, you may have to wage all-out war. Satan wants us to believe that controlling our thoughts is impossible. He wants us to think our attempts will always end in defeat. He will play every dirty trick in the book to make sure we're not successful that first time.

Satan is stronger than we are. If we rely on our own strength, we will surely fail. It's crucial to pray—desperately!—for God's help. Ask Him to enable you, strengthen your tenacity, protect you from the attacks of the enemy, and give you victory over your own mind.

Next, resolve aloud to take whatever time and exert whatever effort is required to completely submit your thoughts to Jesus. A half-hearted resolution will accomplish nothing. When we find ourselves waffling, the best thing to do is to pray as many times as it takes and ask God to strengthen our willpower.

You may have to take an extended lunch. You may need to request a personal day or half-day off from work. You may need to go on a drive or otherwise isolate yourself from people. You will need to make sacrifices to carve out time to do this. But the question is, and always has been, do we value holiness and obedience enough to sacrifice for it?

When submitting our thoughts to Christ, everything should be bathed in prayer. We start by praying. We end by praying. And in between, we pray. Only prayer reinforces our utter dependence on God. This type of dependence wields the shield of faith, which the Bible tells us will extinguish the flaming arrows of the evil one.

Any time the taboo thought surfaces, begin by praying. Don't attempt to hide it from God. He knows it already. He's not your enemy, though Satan will try to tell you He is. God is your ally in this battle.

Read Scripture, journal, listen to music, and in the name of Jesus rebuke the enemy aloud, as the situation requires. It's important to always give priority to the Word of God. This is one of our few offensive weapons against Satan. God promises His Word won't return to Him void without accomplishing exactly what He wants it to.

Let me share an example from my own life. This comes from a fierce battle I experienced in taking thoughts captive. Though it has nothing to do with forgiveness, it gives a glimpse of the prayer we can engage in, the Scriptures we can quote, and the tenacity of the temptations we may face when we're trying to submit our thoughts to God.

I've chosen this particular example because each stage of the battle was so well-documented in my journal. It all started when, for the purity of my thought life, God asked me to stop watching a television show I had enjoyed. My husband, Peter, and I had arrived in Japan as first-time missionaries just a few months earlier.

"Okay, God, here I am in Japan," I prayed. "This is a spiritual battlefield. I will not survive if I maintain pet sins or deny Your right to complete control over my life. I can't afford to give the enemy a foothold."

A furtive whisper came to my ear. "You can always watch the TV show back in Canada when you're out of here."

But doesn't that negate surrender? I thought. *Putting sin in my back pocket for later is still sin. Spiritual warfare isn't any less in Canada; it just takes different forms.*

"God, it's in my head!" I prayed. "I cannot indulge in this, but I'm weak. I feel double-minded. Please help me submit to You."

He brought a verse to mind. "If we confess our sins, He is faithful and righteous to forgive us our sins and to cleanse us from all unrighteousness." (1 John 1:9)

I opened my journal and picked up my pen once more.

October 16, 2011

Okay, God, I confess before You that I have sinned. I've ignored Your prompting to turn off the TV and have wilfully indulged my own desires above Yours. Lord, I give over this area of my life to You. I'm too feeble to break these chains. They feel like an addiction. But, Father, when I am weak You are strong. Please enable me to cast off "what lies behind and…press on toward the goal for the prize of the upward call of God in Christ Jesus" (Philippians 3:13–14).

Lord—that very title means You are my master—please align my will with Yours. Give me peace in my spirit and help me—help me!—I pray, to live a life that's pure and holy in Your sight. Only You can do this. I can't.

"I have been crucified with Christ; and it is no longer I who live, but Christ lives in me; and the life which I now live in the flesh I live by faith in the Son of God, who loved me and gave Himself up for me." (Galatians 2:20)

Okay, God. I won't be fearful about the future and whether I'll be able to withstand temptation. I'm to live by faith in You. I can't hold out, but I can submit myself to You and allow Your Spirit to work through me and resist on my behalf.

I immediately felt a profound sense of freedom.

"Thank You for forgiving me," I prayed. "Thank You for convicting me, though I'd said no to You before."

After this, temptations to dodge around obedience continued to cascade around me. I paced around our apartment, quoting Scripture to myself for several hours to keep them at bay. Eventually, they abated.

Our fight to control our thoughts may be fiercest the first time we attempt to do this. It's no surprise that Satan would love to deceive us into thinking we're slaves to the unpredictability of our own minds.

We may experience raging battles of submission at other times as well. How marvellous that our Saviour, Jesus Christ, has won the war against sin and death and slavery! We are free! We can choose right at the start of a struggle to appropriate His victory on our behalf. God is the source of both our confidence and our later triumph. By faith, we can thank Him in advance for these things.

If we've taken our thoughts captive and decided not to continue memorizing past trauma, we're ready to take action. Over the years, I've discovered several exercises that encourage healing and enable forgiveness. In some situations, it may be necessary to go through each step. In others, only a few may be needed. We should feel free to go through as many or as few as circumstances require. Whatever the case, *dependence on God* is the key. I have never regretted adopting this as my perpetual starting point before acknowledging my pain and rightful position as a servant of God.

I recommend always using the first three exercises. Then, choose from the remaining items and experiment with your own methods based on what's most effective for you.

Acknowledge Your Emotions

When we've been hurt, we may feel grief, pain, anger, or a mixture of all three. It's important to give our feelings space for expression without denying them. Lest we think this approach is not appropriate for the people of God, let us remember that many godly people in the Bible openly expressed themselves.

1. Hannah wept and prayed before the Lord (see 1 Samuel 1:10).

2. Joseph wept copiously before forgiving his brothers (see Genesis 45:2).

3. Moses was so angry with the Israelites that he broke the first set of the Ten Commandments, without incurring any rebuke from God (see Exodus 32:19).

4. David, perhaps one of the most emotive people in the Bible, acknowledged feelings of sorrow, betrayal, and anger when wronged (see Psalm 6, 22, 55, 68, 137, and 143 for examples).

5. Even Jesus wept at points, whether at a funeral or at the thought of the judgment that would one day come against Jerusalem (see John 11:35, Luke 19:41).

Expressing our emotions doesn't mean we wallow or allow ourselves to sin. It does mean we resist the temptation to put a pleasant face on our situation and ignore the bad. Our subconscious selves need us to admit we've been wronged and acknowledge that there are now emotional and spiritual issues to work through.

Without this step, we're emotionally adrift—like a person looking at a map and trying to go somewhere without first taking the time to find his current location. We can't move on before recognizing where we are right now.

Pray

There's something extraordinary and wonderful about prayer. We often hear about the power of prayer and how prayer moves the arm of God. Yet He is not a giant robot in the sky who only acts when we press His prayer button. Prayer is so remarkable because the One we're talking with is remarkable. Whenever a life brushes up against that of the Creator, extraordinary things happen.

God builds a yearning for change into the hearts of His children. If we're Christians, we should want to become more like Jesus. If this desire is weak, perhaps we've been quenching the Holy Spirit. Chances are, somewhere along the way we've felt His prompting towards greater holiness and have ignored Him.

It all comes down to our readiness to submit and obey, our willingness to embrace the plans God has for us, and our openness to being changed. When we've been wounded, it's tough to let go of hurt and consider the perspective of the person or people who have injured us. This is particularly true when the facts of the situation are in dispute. We find it difficult to step into another person's shoes when those shoes have been used to kick us.

We're only ready to be changed when we develop such a craving for healing—such a longing for Jesus—that we're willing to do anything to fulfill it. Then, our gentle Saviour shows us His perspective and primes us to pray for those who have caused our hurt. This is the vehicle God uses to soften our hearts and redefine our situations.

Jesus said, "Love your enemies and pray for those who persecute you" (Matthew 5:44) not only for the good of our enemies but also for our benefit. It's difficult to genuinely plead for someone else's welfare and still carry bitterness in our own hearts.

Be willing to give up pride and the last word

In the previous chapter, we talked about the need to recognize our own sinfulness. An attitude of humility is foundational to our capacity to forgive. The American politician Ezra Taft Benson once said, "Pride is concerned with *who* is right. Humility is concerned with *what* is right." (emphasis mine)

We often become fixated on our rights when we are hurt. We may think forgiving those who have wronged us is synonymous with giving up our liberties. This is a lie—we had no rights in the first place. They are a human construct.

The Bible says all people are slaves—either to sin or to Christ. In ourselves, our only freedom lies in the choice of whom to serve; without Jesus, our only right is the right to go to hell. That is where we end up without grace. When we join

God's family, He gives us the right to be called sons of God. Everything that follows is God's gracious and merciful gift to us. There's a reason Paul tells us to give thanks continually!

In the story of the unmerciful servant, the master expected his servant to extend the same forgiveness he had received. This was non-negotiable. When the servant refused to forgive his co-worker, the master incarcerated him.

Author Roger Campbell notes, "The purpose of this parable is to make clear that when God calls on a member of His kingdom to forgive, He does not call on him to renounce a right, but that he has no right in the matter. By asking for and accepting forgiveness, he has pledged himself to show it."[4]

Japan's tea ceremony is a beautiful ritual that many believe is rooted in Christian theology and practice. Key aspects mimic the sacrament of holy communion. When Christians were persecuted starting in the late sixteenth century, they would secretly meet in tea houses for communion because it was so similar to the tea ceremony that casual observers couldn't tell the difference.[5]

The tea ceremony is practiced by all classes in Japanese society; it is said one must exercise humility to properly carry it out. To access a traditional tearoom, participants must first remove their swords—the ceremony originated during the time of samurai—and come in on their knees. The entryways into these rooms are so low there is no other way to get in.

Likewise, there is only one way to enter the room of emotional freedom—through the door of forgiveness.

"It is a small, narrow door, and cannot be entered without stooping."[6]

Giving up self-regard and the last word requires substantial self-control. We must wilfully 'stoop' our egos and submit them to the Lordship of Jesus Christ. Only then can we take the next step in the journey.

Try to find common ground

When we give up pride, we unleash a host of methods that can help us forgive. One device is finding commonalities between ourselves and those who have hurt us.

The Bible says, "None is righteous, no, not one" (Romans 3:10, ESV), and "There is nothing new under the sun" (Ecclesiastes 1:9). This means there is nothing happening right now that has not happened earlier in history. The sins committed against us have been committed before, against other people.

Every evil against people is also an evil against God, the One who gave life to those people and authored justice. Our pain can teach us something about Him. The Bible tells us:

> God created man in His own image,
> in the image of God He created him;
> male and female He created them.
>
> GENESIS 1:27

Since we were made in God's image, our emotions when betrayed can provide insight into how He feels when we sin against Him. Forgiveness becomes easier when we identify with those who have hurt us and realize we commit the same sins against God that they have committed against us. We recognize our own brokenness in theirs.

For instance, if an old friend has betrayed me, how much more have I betrayed God? If someone has abandoned me, how much more have I abandoned and ignored my heavenly Father? If someone I trusted has taken someone else's side in a conflict, what about the times I've discarded my relationship with Jesus for some lesser thing?

Applying this method may be arduous at first, but with practice it gets easier. To help get the creative juices flowing, here are two further examples to mull over.

When a family member shuts you out from his life

Try asking yourself a series of questions:

- How have I shut God out of my heart?
- When have I been more interested in protecting my own sin than in having a deeper relationship with God?
- When have I been so selfish that I've not given a thought to the hurt I may be causing my heavenly Father?

When someone defrauds you

Consider the following:

- When have I felt entitled to money, power, or positions that weren't mine?

- How have I cheated God of my time, talents, or financial gifts? Have I held back anything that actually belongs to Him?
- When have I allowed fear or arrogance to propel me across the line into sin?

When I come to God with the sins committed against me and ask Him to show me how I've committed those same sins against Him or someone else, I realize I'm no greater than my antagonist. It takes immense courage to be this humble, but I've found no better way to generate long-lasting, genuine forgiveness within my heart.

Such forgiveness comes not from a place of superiority but from a place of recognizing our own sinfulness. We recognize we cannot possibly continue to hold a grudge against someone else when we have treated our Saviour—who is much more worthy of honour than we are!—in a similar fashion.

This approach is marvellous because it feeds:

- repentance and growth towards holiness;
- understanding of the sacrifice Jesus makes when He forgives us;
- gratitude for Jesus' forgiveness; and
- intimacy with our Saviour.

How beautiful that the act of forgiveness can enable us to better love and appreciate our Lord Jesus!

Have compassion

Recognizing the brokenness in other people can sometimes fuel our ability to forgive them. Each of us is damaged in our own way. Unfortunately, hurt is self-propagating. When we are suffering, our attention is pulled towards our own pain, and we're much more likely to lash out at other people. Perhaps the person who has wronged you is broken too.

Some people tend to take on the hurts of those they're close to. They may treat another person's enemies as their own. This results in a form of bondage difficult to shake.

Others may seem hard and impenetrable, but their armour may shield a grave wound sustained long ago. They may have allowed themselves to become brittle and bitter as a mode of self-protection.

Avoid superior attitudes

Whichever methods we employ to aid forgiveness, it's imperative to examine our attitudes and make sure they don't cause us to commit sins of pride or arrogance against those we're attempting to forgive.

If I tend to be arrogant towards hurtful people, I may begin to think of myself as better than they are. I may scorn and pity them from a place of supposed superiority.

Be careful to ensure your own heart is pure and that you're not perpetrating wrongs against those you're trying to forgive. When we ask for His help, God can enlighten our hearts and minds to recognize if this is happening. It may be necessary to go to those who have wronged us and ask for their forgiveness too.

Write it out

Sometimes it's helpful to draft a letter to the person who's caused us hurt, and never send it. This can be particularly effective when that individual is unable or unwilling to admit wrongdoing. It allows us to identify our feelings as legitimate and express them without fear of reprisal or rejection. It also helps us to understand the things we're feeling because the words that flow from our pens often are from some deeper, unknown part of us. After expressing ourselves, we can recognize the other person's brokenness as well as our own and come to a place where we turn this over to the gentle Healer, who enables us to forgive others as He's forgiven us.

I would suggest writing your note by hand. Often the tactile nature of pen, paper, and movement draws things out of the heart that we don't even know are there. Here are a few questions that may help you get started:

- What happened?
- How do you feel?
- How may this situation affect the person who hurt you? (Don't think just of immediate costs but also of future ones.)

- What specific actions and attitudes may you need to forgive?

After you're finished, set up an empty chair. Imagine the hurtful person sitting in front of you. Read the letter aloud to him or her. Take your time. Your pain is legitimate. Don't gloss it over.

When you're done, burn or otherwise destroy the paper so no one else can see it. Treat the destruction of this letter as a proclamation that you will no longer hold that person's wrongs against him or her. The journey of forgiveness is not over, but you have taken the first step.

If it's too traumatic to imagine the person who has wronged you, try reading your note aloud to God. He will always be someone with whom it's safe to share our hurts, because when we're hurting so is He.

Just be sure to destroy all copies when you're done.

Remember to take thoughts captive

Deeper wounds require more time to heal. It will be necessary to continue taking stray thoughts captive throughout this process.

I would recommend memorizing a few Bible verses to help. We never know when the enemy may try to attack, and a physical or electronic book will not always be available. We may have our hands full with children or cooking, driving, or presenting a new business model to a client. However, we can still quote Scripture in our minds to fend off the attacks of the evil one as they happen. The Bible says the Word of God is like a sword. It enables us to parry the enemy's blows. Satan cannot stand long in the presence of Jesus' majesty.

There's another factor in memorization that no one seems to talk about. In my times of deepest crisis, when the pain is so searing it leaves me gasping for air, I turn to the text I can access with my mind, not my fingers. The Scriptures I've memorized are the most meaningful and potent. That's because the act of memorization makes those passages a part of me. Distress dulls the brain, but when I quote the Scriptures aloud, the Holy Spirit enables me to remember the words. He empowers me to wield His sword, and gives me access to His victory.

Satan never wants us to experience a sense of triumph when we're under attack. If we've memorized Scriptures, though, the memorization itself provides a key to defeating our enemy. Here are my favourite go-to verses:

- Galatians 2:20—"I have been crucified with Christ; and it is no longer I who live, but Christ lives in me; and the life which I now live in the flesh I live by faith in the Son of God, who loved me and gave Himself up for me."

- James 4:7—"Submit therefore to God. Resist the devil and he will flee from you."

- 2 Corinthians 10:5—"We are destroying speculations and every lofty thing raised up against the knowledge of God, and we are taking every thought captive to the obedience of Christ."

- Romans 8:37–39—"But in all these things we overwhelmingly conquer through Him who loved us. For I am convinced that neither death, nor life, nor angels, nor principalities, nor things present, nor things to come, nor powers, nor height, nor depth, nor any other created thing, will be able to separate us from the love of God, which is in Christ Jesus our Lord."

- 1 Corinthians 10:13—"No temptation has overtaken you but such as is common to man; and God is faithful, who will not allow you to be tempted beyond what you are able, but with the temptation will provide the way of escape also, so that you will be able to endure it."

- Hebrews 4:15–16—"For we do not have a high priest who cannot sympathize with our weaknesses, but One who has been tempted in all things as we are, yet without sin. Therefore let us draw near with confidence to the throne of grace, so that we may receive mercy and find grace to help in time of need."

- Philippians 1:6—"For I am confident of this very thing, that He who began a good work in you will perfect it until the day of Christ Jesus."

Guard your heart and actively engage

In times of suffering, guarding our hearts is essential. We must not give in to sinning against the people who have sinned against us (see Romans 12:14–21). Denying our longing for righteous vindication is perhaps one of the most difficult things we will ever do. But it is necessary. We don't want to cause the same wounds in innocent people. Remember, there is *always* collateral damage.

It's imperative to keep our hearts humble and seeking Jesus. You and I must resist the urge to gossip and instead find ways to speak kindly about those who have hurt us.[7] Encourage someone else. Reaching outside yourself may be painful at first. You and I have wounds. Jesus can heal them, and He will. The pain will not last forever. But the things we learn in this place—the ways we grow—those things very well may last, if we let them.

Repeat, as necessary

When I was a little girl, I realized I needed to forgive someone who had harmed me. It took a while to do so, but I finally did.

A few weeks later, all the old fury, bitterness, and unforgiveness were back in my heart.

I was so surprised!

I had battled to be godly. I thought I had forgiven this person. How could all the anger be back? Had I been wrong?

Had I not forgiven after all? My torment increased with these questions.

It took me months to realize the truth: forgiveness, particularly when there are deep wounds, is not a onetime event. It is not linear. It's cyclical.

Our feelings of animosity and hurt don't simply evaporate when we decide to forgive. They may very well return. As we sift through the things that have happened, new emotions will often surface. This is not wrong or evil. It's a part of the healing process.

When we gain new insights, our reactions undergo subtle changes and need to be addressed anew. We can't yank out the leech of distress and say forgiveness is complete. We need God to soothe our hearts and ease that pain.[8]

If we want to forgive someone completely, we must adopt attitudes of tenacious grace. As persistent as our bitterness and anger are, godly forgiveness must be twice as adamant. This requires vigilance. In some ways, it's easier to recognize bitterness and anger for what they are when the hurt is fresh. But what about in two years? Five? Ten? Sometimes resentment creeps in so gradually that we don't even notice it.

Our only hope is to submit our hearts to God for cleaning. We cannot afford to become complacent. Every day—or even more frequently—we need to humble ourselves before God and ask Him to examine and cleanse us. This is the only way to remain pliable and saturated with forgiveness and humility rather than becoming brittle and bitter.

Pace yourself

Undertaking the journey of forgiveness can require a lot of courage and hard work. We may sometimes become impatient with the process and wish we could move more quickly. We may become discouraged at times, and even want to quit.

It's necessary to pace ourselves and in doing so view ourselves as whole people, not just a mind or a body or a spirit. All three contribute to who we are, and each one affects the other parts. If we want to become emotionally healthy, it's important not to neglect any one aspect of ourselves.

For deep wounds, don't try to journey towards forgiveness on your own. Develop a support team to give you wise counsel. This may include a fitness buddy who jogs with you and helps you care for your body, a therapist or wise friend to help you take care of your mind, and a prayer partner who will minister to your spiritual self.

Be careful about whom you choose. Search for people with a certain level of maturity, who don't over-spiritualize the world and who aren't judgmental. On the other hand, someone who is a pushover may not provide *enough* support. Be sure to submit your team selection to God and allow Him to direct you to the people who are best suited for your specific needs—even you may not fully understand what they are yet!

Be sure to rest often, stay hydrated, and continually return to your heavenly Father for refreshment and renewal.

Trauma can make us feel separated not only from the love of God but also from feeling at ease in our own skin. We may feel disconnected from ourselves, our purpose, and the value that God places on us. It will take time to repair the damage, but it is possible, and it is worth it.

Forgiveness is not a sprint. It is a marathon.

18
Forgiving Ourselves

> *I don't believe self-forgiveness is possible until we have been forgiven by someone outside ourselves.*
> ROBERT HICKS, AUTHOR AND MILITARY CHAPLAIN

PEOPLE IN OUR SOCIETY SOMETIMES let themselves off the hook too easily. They expect forgiveness without truly repenting, abdicate responsibility for their wrongs, and continue cycles of evil because they're unwilling to face ugly truths about themselves. They get angry and cut off friends who try to call them out on their behaviour. At the slightest hint of disagreement, they say, "How dare you judge me?"

It's essential for us to adopt habits of humble self-examination and hearts receptive to godly and righteous rebuke. Without this, we have no hope of maturing into people with characters that please God. Though it's true we shouldn't judge each other, particularly when we have so many things to fix in our own lives, there is a difference between judgment and accountability. Sadly, many of us now seem unable to distinguish between the two.

Why all this preamble? Simply put, this section on forgiving ourselves is not meant for people who abdicate responsibility. It's for those who admit their wrongdoing but are still caught in infinite loops of shame and guilt.

Most of us experience this type of loop at some point. Perhaps we've repented, sought and received forgiveness, and tried to make amends. We may find it easy to be merciful to others but more difficult to have compassion on ourselves. We're always aware of the sins we've committed, frozen in blocks of guilt that we cannot escape. Perhaps we don't even *want* to be free, because remaining in prison is an effective way to punish ourselves. We deserve to suffer. We know it in our bones.

Such thinking is true—to an extent. We do deserve punishment for our sins. That's the reason Jesus came to die for us on the cross. If we're Christians, we've accepted the reality of our guilt and the need to pay for it. We've also embraced Jesus' sacrifice; He has paid our debt, and we are free.

But now, faced with concrete examples of our sin, we're mired in difficulty. We're unable to let go of those former debts.

Though this mentality *feels* like a humble one, it communicates implicit pride. Through His death on the cross, Jesus Himself has forgiven our sins. The Bible reassures us of this repeatedly. If we refuse to forgive ourselves, we elevate our forgiveness above God's. Though He has pardoned us, we won't do the same for ourselves. We're superior. We know better than God.

When we trace this line of thinking to its conclusion, our decision becomes much more clear cut. Talking myself down from the ledge of guilt gets easier when I ask a simple question: "Am I better than God?"

Our enemy, Satan, would love to keep us trapped by the weight of our sin. Guilt is one of those emotions that can incapacitate us like almost nothing else. If he can keep us mired in shame, he knows we will feel unworthy to do the work God has called us to do. We will remain frozen in time, at the point of our iniquity, unable to go on. Void of victory, we will be incapable of entering the abundance God has planned for us. Satan will win.

Our adversary loves to whisper little messages to our hearts, recalling our sin and telling us it is unforgivable. We can defeat him with the sword of the spirit: the Word of God. Here are a few of my favourite verses to use against such onslaughts.

- 1 John 1:9—"If we confess our sins, He is faithful and righteous to forgive us our sins and to cleanse us from all unrighteousness."

- Romans 8:33–34—"Who will bring a charge against God's elect? God is the one who justifies; who is the one who condemns? Christ Jesus is He who died, yes, rather who was raised, who is at the right hand of God, who also intercedes for us."

- Psalm 103:12—"As far as the east is from the west, so far has He removed our transgressions from us."

- Romans 8:31–32—"What then shall we say to these things? If God is for us, who is against us? He who did not spare His own Son, but delivered Him over for us all, how will He not also with Him freely give us all things?"

- Romans 8:37–39—"But in all these things we overwhelmingly conquer through Him who loved us. For I am convinced that neither death, nor life, nor angels, nor principalities, nor things present, nor things to come, nor powers, nor height, nor depth, nor any other created thing, will be able to separate us from the love of God, which is in Christ Jesus our Lord."

At times, we may be too sick or dizzy to read, or have a brain injury that prevents us from understanding the written word. Satan doesn't ambush us only when it's convenient for us; when we memorize Scripture, we are essentially taking a mini-Bible with us wherever we go. We can meditate on it at any time.

When we marinate ourselves in God's Word, Satan finds it difficult to conquer us. Every time a guilt-laden thought comes to our minds, if we relentlessly quote Scripture, eventually it must disappear. This is part of "taking every thought captive" (2 Corinthians 10:5). We don't have to be slaves to guilt. For however long the onslaught lasts, we can alternate between praying (relying on God) and reciting Scripture (warding off evil and reminding ourselves of what is real). The only way to counter Satan's potent lies is with the mighty truths in God's Word.

It is possible, and we can be victorious.

19

Testing our Forgiveness

Forgiving is love's revolution against life's unfairness. When we forgive, we ignore the normal law that straps us to the natural law of getting even and, by the alchemy of love, we release ourselves from our own painful pasts.

Lewis B. Smedes, author and theologian

When we're hurt, the danger of becoming bitter is high. Continuous, honest self-evaluation is a key counteragent. Certain questions can help test whether forgiveness has taken hold in our hearts. I like to go through them from time to time, especially when dealing with deep hurts, because bitterness can creep in—even years later.

In conducting this evaluation, it's often advisable to get away from normal life for a while. Set aside a morning, an afternoon, or a whole day. Go into nature or a quiet place where distractions are at a minimum—wherever you're able to think best.

Bring a journal. Prepare to pray. Ask God to help you answer these questions[1] with honesty and courage. Be willing to find ugliness within yourself. When you confront those things and submit them to the lordship of Christ, their power will diminish, and you will be able to step into Jesus' victory.

Let's begin.

1. Do I see myself as superior to, or on an equal playing field with, the person who has hurt me?

We often feel powerless when hurt. Our sense of well-being and control evaporates. The human psyche, however, finds creative ways to reassert power—sometimes through criticism. At first, this may be confined to the individual who has wounded us, but eventually a critical attitude will expand to tear down even those we love and respect. Ungodly choices don't remain isolated. We may end up wronging not only the person who has mistreated us but also innocent people. Fault-finding attitudes have no place in the life of a loving Christ-follower.

Martin Luther King Jr. once said, "I have begun to realize how hard it is for a lot of people to think about living without someone to look down upon, really look down upon. It is not that they will feel cheated out of someone to hate, it is that they will be compelled to look more closely at themselves, at what they don't like in themselves…someday all of us will see that when we start going after a race or religion, a type, a region, a section of the Lord's humanity—then we're cutting into His heart, and we're bleeding badly ourselves."[2]

Looking down on other people can be an addiction. It perversely feeds our sense of pride. Jesus once told His disciples a story about a Pharisee and a tax collector:

> Two men went up into the temple to pray, one a Pharisee and the other a tax collector. The Pharisee stood and was

praying this to himself: 'God, I thank You that I am not like other people: swindlers, unjust, adulterers, or even like this tax collector. I fast twice a week; I pay tithes of all that I get.' But the tax collector, standing some distance away, was even unwilling to lift up his eyes to heaven, but was beating his breast, saying, 'God, be merciful to me, the sinner!' I tell you, this man went to his house justified rather than the other; for everyone who exalts himself will be humbled, but he who humbles himself will be exalted.

LUKE 18:10–14

Filled with pride, we become the Pharisee scorning the tax collector. By having someone to spurn, by having someone lower on the totem pole, we think we somehow commend ourselves to God. We are more lovable, more 'worthy' of His attention. But at the end of the parable, Jesus said it was the tax collector—not the Pharisee—who went on his way, forgiven.

The Pharisee never asked for forgiveness. He only thanked God there was someone to look down on.

How interesting that *God fulfilled the desires of both men.* The tax collector's prayer for forgiveness was granted. The Pharisee was thankful for someone to look down upon, and his wish was also satisfied. There will always be someone new whom we can creatively diminish.

A critical attitude is like a wild cat. At first, we may think we have it under control, but soon it escapes, and we realize it was never tame in the first place. It bides its time and ultimately turns against us. The thing that helped us gain a sense of control—criticism—soon shows its true nature and delivers us into the clutches of bitterness. In the end, we're at its mercy, again miserable and powerless—perhaps even more so than before!

Now we have a choice. We can continue to wilfully engage in sinful, critical attitudes, or we can repent and run back to the arms of Jesus. If we choose Jesus, He pulls out the weeds of bitterness by their roots and allows our hearts' gardens to flourish and grow once more.

2. Am I able to discuss what has happened without wanting revenge?

When faced with injustice, we may experience anger even after forgiving. This is natural, though our desire for vengeance should evaporate over time.

Sometimes the cycle of forgiveness may never be completed. In one case, when I think about a certain insidious evil that touched my life, I no longer feel furious on my own behalf. I may feel sad for my younger self and for the cost the wrongdoers have now paid for their sins. But there is no outrage, no bitterness. Yet, when I remember the destruction those same people enacted against others, I may still become angry. Wounds cut deep to the cores of those other people too. They're still suffering. I have to make a conscious decision to forgive every time I think about what happened.

Sometimes I still get indignant, but my desire for vengeance is gone. I no longer thirst for justice. God has taken care of me and the others. He's protected us from being destroyed. I know that if a penalty is required, He will administer it. If none comes, I trust that God in His wisdom will use whatever happens for the benefit of His kingdom and the glory of His name.

If you or I have not forgiven someone, our sense of injustice is piqued every time we think of them going about their lives without being punished. If we have forgiven, we can leave justice in God's hands. We have no desire to dictate to Him what justice is and how it should be applied.

Forgiveness means we are content with our Father's decisions concerning those who have wronged us. If He decides to bless them, we trust He is right. Our sense of well-being is not connected to their level of distress.

3. Have I taken responsibility for my wrongdoing in this situation?

When hurt, we often feel that blame rests squarely at the feet of the person who has caused our pain. In some cases, this is true. Yet, we are human. We are sinful. Sometimes, we share responsibility. Even when most of the blame lies with the other party, we always have something we can confess and repent. It's necessary to examine our own hearts to root out unrighteousness, no matter what the circumstances.

At times, our guilt stems from an action. At other times, it may come from an attitude.

We may be largely innocent and may not have caused the situation. Still, there's always something we can repent of—even if it's the sin of feeling proud or superior to the one who has hurt us. If we are to genuinely forgive, we must be willing to humble ourselves and seek God's pardon for our own sinfulness.

4. Am I able to thank God for the things I've learnt?

There's something about gratitude that helps banish bitterness. It's hard to resent something when we're somehow grateful for it.

One of the most effective ways to engage in forgiveness is to build on a foundation of redemption.

In my early adulthood, I walked away from following Jesus. After the abuse in my childhood, I'd finally had enough of suffering. *God hasn't protected me*, I thought. *I could do better by myself.*

After a few years on my own, I realized that the misery of my life had not improved but had worsened many times over. I repented of my former attitudes and returned to Jesus.

Upon my return, I decided to approach suffering differently. If I could learn from hardship and use it to help someone else in the future, I could be grateful for it.

When we recognize how God is using a painful situation for both the good of His kingdom and our own personal good, our hearts are unlocked to experience joy.

Jesus said, "Rejoice and be glad, for your reward in heaven is great" (Matthew 5:12). The joy Jesus talked about is not a feeling disingenuous to our state. Rather, it transcends circumstances and is birthed from trust in God.

This joy is based on a reality that our eyes can't always see: God is at work along many dimensions. He is using even painful situations to grow us into the people we want to be—people who swim in those deep pools of Living Water that refresh, restore, and transform us to be more like our beloved Jesus.

5. Am I able to do good to those who have caused me pain?

Jesus told His followers to love their enemies, pray for those who persecuted them, and do good to those who hated them. Behaviour like this is only possible with a genuine, forgiving spirit. Three Old Testament characters serve as role models in this.

Samuel (1 Samuel 12)

God appointed the prophet Samuel to lead the people of Israel. Samuel experienced many a hurt at the hands of the Israelites. Sometimes they ignored him. At other times, they outright rejected him as their leader and God as their ruler.

They demanded a king so they could be like the other nations. God granted their request. They would live to regret it. The fickle nature of human rulers can lead to much suffering.

When they realized their mistake, the Israelites repented. The prophet reassured them that if they continued to follow God, they would be all right.

"Far be it from me that I should sin against the Lord by ceasing to pray for you," he said (1 Samuel 12:23). Samuel recognized that ceasing to intercede for the people of Israel would be a form of bearing a grudge for their rejection. He knew a life that honours God is characterized by forgiveness.

Job (Job 1–2; 42:7–17)

The sufferings of Job are legendary and the source of an English idiom: we talk about having 'the patience of Job' during trials. Job started off with vast wealth and a large family. For no known reason, he experienced the sudden loss of all his possessions, the lives of his children, and eventually his health and marital unity.

Like Samuel, Job suffered at human hands. His 'friends' thought his hardship was God's punishment for sin. They blamed him for his own suffering.

Job's friends caused deep emotional pain. Yet, when everything was over, he prayed for their welfare. The Bible tells us God responded to the purity of Job's heart. He not only accepted Job but also restored and doubled his former wealth, and provided him with more children. From then on, no one could doubt that Job was a servant of the living God. He was vindicated.

Joseph (Genesis 37–50)

Jealous and resentful of their adolescent sibling, Joseph's brothers sold him into slavery. In those days, a slave's lifespan was short. Joseph's brothers thought they could make some money from his suffering and death.

Joseph spent years in the house of a man called Potiphar, the captain of the Egyptian Pharaoh's bodyguards. He was falsely accused of attempting to rape Potiphar's wife and was thrown into prison for more than two years. There, Joseph demonstrated a God-given ability to interpret dreams.

When Pharaoh had nightmares and required an explanation that no one else could supply, he turned to Joseph, who predicted a severe famine. In response, Pharaoh elevated Joseph to second in command over all Egypt.

Can you imagine how Potiphar and his wife must have felt when Joseph was promoted? I'm sure there was quite a bit of trembling in that household!

That was nothing compared to the reaction of Joseph's brothers when they realized they were begging bread from the man they had sold to foreign tradesmen.

The Bible indicates that Joseph didn't take revenge on his brothers. Instead, he tested whether they had changed. When it was obvious they had, Joseph welcomed his relatives into the land of Egypt, blessed them with extravagant gifts, and relocated them, so they and their families could live close to him.

Joseph's forgiveness was extraordinary. After their father died, the brothers were so sure Joseph would retaliate that they begged him for their lives.

Joseph wept on hearing this. He realized the burden of guilt and fear his siblings had been carrying since they'd moved to Egypt. He responded, "Don't be afraid of me. Am I God, that I can punish you? You intended to harm me, but God intended it all for good. He brought me to this position so I could save the lives of many people. No, don't be afraid. I will continue to take care of you and your children." (Genesis 50:19–21, NLT)

Our siblings are supposed to love and look out for us. They're supposed to have our backs through life's most difficult situations. How was Joseph able to forgive his brothers? He probably started by forgiving lesser sins.

If I were to speculate, I would say Joseph didn't take retribution on Potiphar either. He likely forgave the man who was deceived into thinking Joseph had tried to rape his wife—and the woman who, out of wounded pride and malice, sent him to prison. Perhaps those smaller decisions enabled Joseph to tackle the mammoth task of forgiving his own brothers.

Our whole lives are a training ground. The choices we make today influence the decisions of tomorrow. If we forgive now, forgiveness later becomes a little easier.

We must each consider what sort of people we want to become. We can walk down the path that leads further and further into bitterness until all that's left is putrid, or we can choose the way that repays evil with good and that thanks God for the blessings He can bring even out of horrendous circumstances.

20

Things That Make Forgiveness Harder

> *True forgiveness costs.*
> ROBERT HICKS, AUTHOR AND MILITARY CHAPLAIN

So, we've decided to forgive. The process may be long and onerous. Certain factors may make forgiveness still more arduous. If we're not expecting them, surprise can intensify our difficulty.

1. THE PERSON IS STILL WRONGING US.

If we want to follow in Jesus' footsteps even when we're in the midst of a situation where someone is still hurting us, we cannot afford to wait until everything is over before we forgive.[1]

We've already talked about Jesus' prayer at the end of His life: "Father, forgive them" (Luke 23:34). Were we to imagine ourselves on the cross as Jesus, the most charitable of us might pray this after everything was finished—perhaps in a saintly display of holiness right before we perished. But Jesus did this *while* He was being crucified. He didn't wait until after He was resurrected. Nor did He hold back until just before He died. He prayed as the soldiers were dividing His clothes, *while He was still suffering*. Jesus chose to forgive when His enemies were still causing Him pain.

We open ourselves to seeds of bitterness if we wait to forgive. Those seeds don't wait for the hurt to end before they sprout in our hearts. If sin doesn't tarry, neither should righteousness.

Remember, Jesus was human and God. He experienced all the same emotions we do. From a human point of view, if we've not forgiven someone ourselves, we're unlikely to solicit pardon on that person's behalf. It's a sure sign of forgiveness when we wholeheartedly work for the benefit of someone who has hurt us. When Jesus solicited God's forgiveness for the soldiers, this was proof that He had forgiven them Himself.

Jesus forgave early. So must we.

2. The person who has wronged us takes our forgiveness for granted.

Sometimes Christians assume it's their right to be forgiven, no matter what they do. The shameless presumption of this attitude sets my teeth on edge. When this happens, the forgiveness required of us expands to cover:

- the original wrongdoing, and
- the new, presumptive stance.

Once more, you and I can find help in humility. When we examine our own hearts, we soon find similar attitudes towards God. This similarity can once again fuel repentance and enable us to share His forgiveness.

I once came across a statement most recently attributed to German poet and writer Heinrich Heine on his deathbed: "Of course God will forgive me; that's His job."[2] This sickening attitude diminishes God to a clerk, rubber-stamping forgiveness for all.

Yet Scottish evangelist and teacher Oswald Chambers warns us to "beware of the pleasant view of the Fatherhood of God—God is so kind and loving that of course He will forgive us. That sentiment has no place whatever in the New Testament. The only ground on which God can forgive us is the tremendous tragedy of the Cross of Christ; to put forgiveness on any other ground is blasphemy. The only ground on which God can forgive sin and reinstate us in His favour is through the Cross of Christ, and in no other way. Forgiveness, which is so easy for us to accept, cost the agony of Calvary."[3]

How many times have we approached God's forgiveness lightly? How many times have we sinned with the implicit assumption that when we're finally ready to repudiate our sin, God will be there to forgive us because it's "His job"?

To my shame, my own answer is, "Too many; I cannot count them."

It's unpleasant to have our forgiveness taken for granted. How galling it must be for Jesus to experience this at our hands. As much as our forgiveness costs us something, Jesus' cost Him much more. When we belittle that price, we wrong our Saviour.

3. WE ADOPT RACIST OR PREJUDICED ATTITUDES.

Our minds try to make sense of hurts we encounter. We often search for the 'otherness' in the people who have wounded us. If we can find some difference between us and them, perhaps we can explain the pain they have caused.

During one period in my life, I was hurt by people who were a different nationality from me. We will call them 'Svegedinians'. These people were Christians, so that couldn't be what made them different. Subconscious reasoning said their culture must have contributed to their hurtful behaviours. My tendency was to think poorly of all Svegedinians.

It's true that sometimes cultural misunderstandings play a role in creating hurt, but often there are other layers to a problem. Fortunately, I recognized what was going on in my spirit towards Svegedinians. With Jesus' help, I was able to take these thoughts captive and regain a God-honouring spiritual and emotional equilibrium.

Our minds were created to make sense of the world we inhabit, but we have to accept that some wounds are senseless. Sometimes we are injured, through no fault of our own, simply because people are sinful. When we recognize this, we see that perhaps we too have hurt someone for the same reason, because we are sinful.

Racism and prejudice can take on lives of their own. This may happen at any time—when wounds are fresh or when scars are mostly healed. If we detect discrimination within ourselves, we can either shrug it off or treat it for what it is—a symptom of sin and unforgiveness.

We can prevent hurt from morphing into racism and prejudice by stubbornly forgiving those who wound us. It is the only way to remain gentle people who don't perpetuate suffering in innocent bystanders.

Closing Part V

Food for Thought

RESEARCH PSYCHOLOGISTS DANIEL KAHNEMAN AND Amos Tversky reached the top of their field in studying cognitive biases, and many believe they came up with their best ideas when they worked together. Their work garnered the Nobel Prize, MacArthur Genius Grant, and the Grawemeyer Award, but in the end their alliance fell apart. Their relational problems stemmed from the same biases they had spent their lives pondering.[1]

This highlights an important truth in the interaction between subjective reality, conflict, forgiveness, and humility.

> The study of cognitive biases cannot help us avoid them. It can only alert us to ways in which we might be wrong.

Doctors Kahneman and Tversky were highly educated, intelligent men, but even they were not immune to the effects of their field. This story puts the truth on display: humility, not study, is the key to forgiveness and conflict resolution. It doesn't matter how much we know about bias, psychology, or the mind. Knowledge is only useful if it feeds humility.

I love that Jesus doesn't leave us to our own devices after He imparts His salvation to us. It's an ongoing work. Just as we keep sinning—even when we don't want to!—He keeps saving us. Through the Holy Spirit, He bestows on us the strength to resist temptation, the capacity to praise and glorify Him amid adversity, and even the ability to obey Him. We need only surrender ourselves into His keeping.

Sometimes the word 'surrender' can be so daunting, can't it? Our struggles to submit feel gargantuan. But the Christian life is simple and beautiful, if we only let it be so.

At times, we take far too much credit for our own virtue. When we give responsibility for our godliness over to Jesus and allow Him to have final say, our lives don't get harder, as Satan would have us believe. They get easier! Jesus enables us to follow Him—not in our own strength but in His!

> We have been crucified with Christ; and it is no longer we who live, but Christ lives in us; and the lives which we now live in the flesh we live by faith in the Son of God, who loved us and gave Himself up for us.
>
> GALATIANS 2:20, MY PARAPHRASE

Going Deeper

1. How is pride the enemy of forgiveness? How does giving up our pride enable us to forgive?

2. Memorize a couple of verses that give you assurance of God's forgiveness after you repent. Remember to keep them fresh in your memory to help you deal with shame and guilt.

3. Why do we sometimes adopt critical attitudes towards other people? List several possibilities.

4. Meditate on 1 Thessalonians 5:18:

    "Give thanks in all circumstances; for this is God's will for you in Christ Jesus" (NIV).

    What can you thank God for, even when you've been hurt?

Part VI

Extraordinary Forgiveness

God sometimes calls us out of normality and onto an extraordinary plane. In this section, let's touch on a few types of forgiveness beyond the ordinary.

We will examine Jesus' command to love our enemies. This is almost an oxymoron—after all, our enemies usually hate us. Yet, following Jesus' way means we're expected to counter evil with good. This uncommon approach is our mandate.

We'll also discuss certain forms of radical forgiveness that are not appropriate in every situation. May we prayerfully consider each one and allow the Holy Spirit to convict and challenge us in our own journeys. Only He has the wisdom to know when these forms should be engaged, and how.

Let's continue.

21

Love Your Enemies

But if your enemy is hungry, feed him, and if he is thirsty, give him a drink.

ROMANS 12:20

THE EXPERIENCE OF OPPRESSION AND exploitation can lead to an intense thirst for justice that becomes so sharp it transforms into a physical sensation. Even so, we need to be vigilant in guarding our hearts. It's easy to sin against people who have wronged us.

Even when engaging in no overt misconduct, we may still foster evil attitudes. No iniquity is hidden from God. He sees it all, including the sins we secretly cultivate.

A person's character is most evident in his private reaction to the downfall of his enemies. The Bible addresses this behaviour in several places. For instance, Proverbs 24:17 says, "Do not gloat when your enemy falls; when they stumble, do not let your heart rejoice" (NIV).

The wise are especially careful when an adversary encounters consequences or discipline. In Ezekiel 25–26, God gave prophecies of judgment and destruction against five nations. Three of them were penalized not for their actions but for their attitudes. They had rejoiced in the downfall of God's chosen people and exulted in Israel's disgrace. They'd said, "Aha!…now that she lies in ruins I will prosper" (Ezekiel 26:2, NIV).

What was true in Ezekiel's time is true now: we must never exult in the judgment and punishment of God's people, regardless of the deeds that might have led them to such a fate. Instead, we should mourn with godly humility when hardship overtakes our enemies. The consequences they now experience result from a situation that brings God distress. Those repercussions are the outcome of disobedience and dishonour brought to His name.

If we take pleasure in the results, we're playing on the same field as the devil and his demons. They, too, revel in God's pain. They hate Him and are His enemies. When we rejoice in things that cause God pain, we become His enemies too. In other words, if we celebrate the downfall of people God loves, we are partying with the demons.

How carefully and humbly we must guard our hearts, particularly in the face of injustice!

Jesus and the Jews of His day knew about hardship. Their nation had been conquered by Rome, stripped of its sovereignty, and forced to live under an oppressive regime. One day, the Jewish people approached Jesus, requesting a sign from heaven. Westerners usually interpret this passage as meaning the Jews were asking Jesus to perform another miracle, to prove He was the Messiah.

For the Jews, a 'sign from heaven' was a euphemism for the destruction of ungodly gentiles.[1] God had given a few signs from heaven in Old Testament times. These included sending fire and brimstone on Sodom and Gomorrah and throwing stones from above at the Hebrews' foes.

The Jewish people believed the Messiah would one day bring judgment upon their enemies and annihilate those who opposed Him. Their request for a sign from heaven was born of a belief that their Saviour would liberate them from Roman rule. If Jesus was the Messiah, He would take out the Romans and free the Jews from tyranny.[2]

> As the crowds were increasing, [Jesus] began to say, "This generation is a wicked generation; it seeks for a sign, and yet no sign will be given to it but the sign of Jonah. For just as Jonah became a sign to the Ninevites, so will the Son of Man be to this generation.
>
> "The Queen of the South will rise up with the men of this generation at the judgment and condemn them, because she came from the ends of the earth to hear the wisdom of Solomon; and behold, something greater than Solomon is here.
>
> "The men of Nineveh will stand up with this generation at the judgment and condemn it, because they

repented at the preaching of Jonah; and behold, something greater than Jonah is here."

LUKE 11:29–32

Jesus promised His countrymen only the sign of Jonah, which has two possible interpretations:

1. The prophet was expelled from the belly of the whale after three days (foreshadowing Jesus' resurrection after three days), and

2. The Ninevites repented when confronted with God's impending judgment for their sins (indicating the future repentance of the gentiles).[3]

In this passage, Jesus concentrated on the second aspect. The Bible tells us repentance is a gift granted by God, who loves all people equally and gives even our enemies opportunities to see the error of their ways.

This teaching still applies today. The godly exercise caution in their desire for justice. When we seek judgment against others, we may become blinded to our own iniquity, sink deep into its mire, and end up being judged *by* those same people!

"Therefore let anyone who thinks that he stands take heed lest he fall." (1 Corinthians 10:12, ESV)

Love Your Enemies

We may sin against our foes in both action and attitude. Thus far, we've focussed on attitudes. They're of primary concern, because outward deeds usually begin with an underlying mindset.

At times, we may have the opportunity to stand up for ourselves and take vengeance on our enemies. Yet, Psalm 7:3–5 says:

> O Lord my God…if there is injustice in my hands,
> If I have rewarded evil to my friend,
> Or have plundered him who without cause was my adversary,
> Let the enemy pursue my soul and overtake it;
> And let him trample my life down to the ground
> And lay my glory in the dust.
> *Selah.*

This passage says if we plunder those who without cause are our enemies, we deserve judgment. 'Plunder' is an old-fashioned term these days. It brings to mind pirates sailing the seven seas, in search of hapless ships full of treasure. The idea of 'plunder' involves taking someone else's possessions by force, whether in war or a raid.[4]

It doesn't matter if we deserve our enemies' hatred or not. We are not to take vengeance on them. Jesus reinforced this teaching when He said, "Do not resist an evil person; but whoever slaps you on your right cheek, turn the other to him also. If anyone wants to sue you and take your shirt, let him have your coat also." (Matthew 5:38–40)

If our conflict is with fellow Christians, the Bible issues an additional caution. It is wrong for Christians to litigate against other Christians (see 1 Corinthians 6:1–8). If we engage in lawsuits against believers, we're essentially plundering one another. Our actions beg God to judge us. I think you and I would agree we never want to wind up in such a precarious position!

The journey towards loving those who have wronged us is certainly a rocky one. There's something profound about the hurt we encounter from those we've opened our hearts to, from those we've selflessly served, from those we've admired and respected and called 'friend'. We may now suffer because of a sin, an attitude, a careless word, or a chain reaction that has caused horrors we never would have foreseen. This place of pain is lonesome—especially when former friends have become our enemies.

Jesus is not a distant God. He's not indifferent to our misery. He has experienced affliction too. And He continues to experience it. When we are wounded and alone, we need only glance over our shoulder to see Jesus beside us. He is going through this with us. When we embrace Him and enter into communion with Him, the fellowship of His suffering is sweet and precious. It is the key to moving us towards loving those we forgive.

At one point I had difficulty forgiving people who had betrayed and abused me. One day, I came to Psalm 51 in my devotions. I didn't get far in praying for God's cleansing before He stopped me. As quickly as thoughts and prayers came into my mind, they dissipated—like watching a video of the ripples on a pond after rocks had been thrown in, at double or triple speed. The mental undulations became smaller and smaller.

"Be still," God said.

It was a weird experience. When He'd asked me to be still in the past, I'd felt filled with His love, united with Him. But this time was different. I was still, and my thoughts were largely empty. I sensed He was with me and I was safe, but I also had the impression of separateness, as if He were across the room.

In the stillness, the pain from my emotional wounds evaporated.

My thoughts flitted around, quickly pulled away, and quieted.

"I'm not very good at thinking about nothing. Can I think about Jesus?"

"Yes."

I thought about Jesus with the children, Jesus on the cross, Jesus living His life. I didn't know what He looked like. I imagined Him with a beard and without, fat, thin.

"I would have loved You any way You looked."

I thought back to Psalm 51. "Please give me a clean heart."

"You are clean," He said.

A pause.

"Lord, I don't just want to be empty of sin. I want to be full of You."

Immediately, I felt joined with Him, as if a pitcher of His love and Spirit had been poured into my soul. We were together again; there was no separateness.

But then I noticed something. The emotional ache was back, deep in my belly.

"Why is the pain back?" I asked. "When we were separate, it was gone. But when You filled me, it came back."

I paused. "Is this Your pain, Jesus? Your pain over what they've done?"

"Yes."

"Is this the way to have compassion on them, to have a godly attitude towards them? To feel Your pain?"

"Yes."

When we feel Jesus' distress and recognize His love towards those who've caused it, we experience not only the fellowship of His suffering but also the fellowship of His love for our enemies. In the end, Jesus provides us with only one way to deal with our foes. We do this with neither hatred nor retribution, for one day they may rise and attack us again. No, our ammunition is much more catastrophic. It's the way Jesus Himself used. It's the way of love. As Martin Luther King Jr. once wrote:

> Far from being the pious injunction of a Utopian dreamer, the command to love one's enemy is an absolute necessity for our survival. Love even for our enemies is the key to the solution of the problems of our world. Jesus is not an impractical idealist; he is the practical realist.
>
> Returning hate for hate multiplies hate, adding deeper darkness to a night already devoid of stars. Darkness cannot drive out darkness; only light can do that. Hate cannot drive out hate; only love can do that. Hate multiplies hate, violence multiplies violence, and toughness multiplies toughness in a descending spiral of destruction.
>
> Love is the only force capable of transforming an enemy into a friend. We never get rid of an enemy by meeting hate with hate; we get rid of an enemy by getting rid of enmity. By its very nature, hate destroys and tears down; by its very nature, love creates and builds up. Love transforms with redemptive power.[5]

In His Sermon on the Mount, Jesus said, "But I say to you who hear, love your enemies, do good to those who hate you, bless those who curse you, pray for those who abuse you" (Luke 6:27–28, ESV). Though He preached a gospel of peace, Jesus' teachings included an explicit assumption that His followers would be hated for His sake. He outlined the approach we should take as our foes' hatred intensifies:

Their behaviour	Our behaviour
They hate	We do good
They curse	We bless
They persecute	We pray

We may think this passage is a mandate to start out strong but temper our reactions if our enemies' antagonism continues to intensify.[6] Don't be fooled. Physical reality is not always a reliable indicator of what's going on in the spiritual world. As human beings, we often place more importance on things we can see than on things we can't. That's why we struggle to pray but find it easier to volunteer at a soup kitchen. The person who prays may seem more passive, but that's only the outward, physical reality. In the spiritual world, a praying Christian arrays herself in armour and wages war against the enemy. Our reactions may become less visible, but they take the battle further into the spiritual realm.

Jesus taught that our love should be intense from the beginning, hoping to turn foes into friends. Like those of our enemies, our responses ramp up as conflict escalates. Since praying is the single most powerful thing we can do, when we devote our entire focus to praying in the final step, exciting things happen! We can only defeat hatred with love by being proactive, not reactive. Jesus provided the perfect example; the Bible tells us He died for us while we were still His enemies.

At one point shortly after my mother was diagnosed with cancer, a family friend who had lived a hard life became offended at the fact that I had been designated the communications liaison for our family through that time. She went on the attack, and I was the target.

I was already overwhelmed by being in Japan, so far away from my family during COVID, with little chance of getting back to see my mum. I thought the best thing to do was to continue giving this person, whom I'll call Millie, updates as they were available and refuse to be baited into responding to her accusations. *If things get too bad*, I told myself, *I can always block her and simply send her one-way updates without seeing her responses.*

I worked hard to cleanse my heart of bitterness and to forgive the attacks she levelled my way at such a vulnerable time.

But one day, a few weeks later, I read that passage from Luke 6 again. As I meditated on Jesus' directive to "do good to those who hate you", I realized I couldn't just leave her alone. I had to do more.

Before I could talk myself out of it, I went online and found a nice floral bouquet.

"Dear Millie," I wrote, "here are some flowers to brighten your day."

Much as I would have liked to sign the card with "Love, Valerie", I knew from sad experience that statements of love could be attacked. So, I simply signed my name and hoped that the act of sending the flowers would communicate the love I had so wanted to express.

The flowers were delivered, and I braced for a response.
Nothing.
No attack, no thank you. Nothing.

I deeply hope that those flowers helped Millie to realize that love was available to her, despite her behaviour. She didn't have to manipulate or cajole to get it. It simply existed, free for her to receive. Perhaps one day I'll get to tell her how loved she is. But in the meantime, I will pray.

If Jesus disowned us the way we may discard our adversaries, the world would be a very different place right now. In my case, I would be wasting away in the decay of my own spiritual and emotional disease, possibly dead, probably mutilated, and definitely miserable. Instead, Jesus has clothed me in His robes of righteousness and redeemed me from that former misery.

Together, let's be instruments of the same love and tenderness Jesus has shown us. We are broken vessels. But 'broken' does not mean 'useless'. When we allow Jesus' glory to shine through our cracks, it can touch and heal our friends and foes and bring many into His rivers of abundance and life.

22

Standing in the Gap

But God demonstrates His own love toward us, in that while we were yet sinners, Christ died for us.

Romans 5:8

THERE IS A FORM OF FORGIVENESS that God never commands us to enact. It's an extraordinary, completely-impossible-for-us-as-human-beings type of forgiveness that we may rarely or never apply. The Bible calls it 'standing in the gap'.

In the passage below, the Lord spoke to His prophet Ezekiel when the people of Israel had turned from Him and were committing great evil. Here are Ezekiel's words.

> And the word of the Lord came to me, saying, "Son of man, say to [Israel], 'You are a land that is not cleansed or rained on in the day of indignation.' There is a conspiracy of her prophets in her midst like a roaring lion tearing the prey. They have devoured lives; they have taken treasure and precious things; they have made many widows in the midst of her. Her priests have done violence to My law and have profaned My holy things; they have made no distinction between the holy and the profane, and they have not taught the difference between the unclean and

the clean; and they hide their eyes from My sabbaths, and I am profaned among them. Her princes within her are like wolves tearing the prey, by shedding blood and destroying lives in order to get dishonest gain. Her prophets have smeared whitewash for them, seeing false visions and divining lies for them, saying, 'Thus says the Lord God,' when the Lord has not spoken. The people of the land have practiced oppression and committed robbery, and they have wronged the poor and needy and have oppressed the sojourner without justice.

"I searched for a man among them who would build up the wall and *stand in the gap* before Me for the land, so that I would not destroy it; but I found no one.

"Thus I have poured out My indignation on them; I have consumed them with the fire of My wrath; their way I have brought upon their heads," declares the Lord God.

EZEKIEL 22:23–31, EMPHASIS MINE

Despite all of Israel's sins, God was ready to forgo destroying the land if someone was willing to stand in the gap for it. This was the only thing that would have made a difference to the fate of Israel. God searched but found no one to do this. So, He poured out His wrath.

Standing in the gap is not an ordinary form of intercession. Scripture never records God condemning anyone for *not* engaging in this extraordinary type of forgiveness. That's because it's also dangerous. It should never be considered lightly. In this passage, not even Ezekiel stood in the gap for Israel. He faced no chastisement or condemnation for this decision.

Standing in the gap goes above and beyond the call of duty. Only three people in the entire Bible did this for the sake of those guilty before God. Let's examine their stories and see what we can learn about what it means to stand in the gap for someone else.

Moses

I wouldn't wish Moses' job on my worst enemy. The people of Israel were hard to lead! They were stubborn. They were ungrateful. They were violent. They threatened Moses' life.

By the time we pick up the story, Israel had grumbled before the Red Sea, complained about water *twice*, and whined about dietary selection.

Moses had just fasted and prayed for forty days and nights on the top of a mountain while God gave him the Ten Commandments on stone tablets. He was tired. Hungry.

The Israelites didn't care. Selfish and oblivious, they reverted to their old habits. They strayed away from the God who had rescued them from Egyptian tyranny.

While Moses was still on the mountain, God told him what was happening below. Here's a snippet of that conversation.

> Then the Lord spoke to Moses, "Go down at once, for your people, whom you brought up from the land of

Egypt, have corrupted themselves. They have quickly turned aside from the way which I commanded them. They have made for themselves a molten calf, and have worshipped it and have sacrificed to it and said, 'This is your god, O Israel, who brought you up from the land of Egypt!'"

The Lord said to Moses, "I have seen this people, and behold, they are an obstinate people. Now then let Me alone, that My anger may burn against them and that I may destroy them; and I will make of you a great nation."

Then Moses entreated the Lord his God, and said, "O Lord, why does Your anger burn against Your people whom You have brought out from the land of Egypt with great power and with a mighty hand? Why should the Egyptians speak, saying, 'With evil intent He brought them out to kill them in the mountains and to destroy them from the face of the earth'?

"Turn from Your burning anger and change Your mind about doing harm to Your people. Remember Abraham, Isaac, and Israel, Your servants to whom You swore by Yourself, and said to them, 'I will multiply your descendants as the stars of the heavens, and all this land of which I have spoken I will give to your descendants, and they shall inherit it forever.'"

Exodus 32:7–13

In this exchange, Moses knew very well *why* God was angry. Still, he requested mercy for a people who had no mercy on him. He reminded God of His reputation among the nations and His vow to Abraham, Isaac, and Jacob. That covenant could still have been fulfilled were God to destroy the people and make of Moses' descendants a great nation; Moses had also descended from Abraham, Isaac, and Jacob. However, he abandoned personal ambition in favour of something greater.

When Moses came down the mountain—from a literal and figurative 'high'—he found the Israelites partying. Were they celebrating his return? Were they praising the God who had saved them?

No. They'd built for themselves a new idol. They were worshipping the statue of the golden calf. The ringleader at the centre of it all was Moses' own brother.

Everything was as God had described it. Overcome with anger, the prophet threw down the stone tablets, which broke.

I would imagine Moses could hardly keep his eyes open when his first marathon meeting with God on the mountain was over. Yet, he did not allow exhaustion to stop him from fasting and praying for an additional forty days and nights on Israel's behalf.

The Psalms record Moses' actions in this way:

> Therefore God said that He would destroy them,
> Had not Moses His chosen one *stood in the breach* before
>   Him,
> To turn away His wrath from destroying them.
>
> PSALM 106:23, EMPHASIS MINE

Standing in the breach is equivalent to standing in the gap.

When Moses interceded on behalf of the people, he didn't offer a few half-hearted prayers. He begged God to forgive Israel's sins and went one step further than anyone before. He prayed:

> "But now, if You will, forgive their sin—and if not, please blot me out from Your book which You have written!"
>
> EXODUS 32:32

Read that prayer again. Let it blow you away.

When they die, people whose names are written in the Book of Life will go to heaven to spend eternity with God. Everyone else will be separated from God forever. In his appeal, Moses requested that he be assigned the same fate as the Israelites. If God was going to send the people to hell for their sin, Moses asked to also be sent there. The prophet actually tied his future to Israel's.

That's love!

And that is standing in the gap.

JESUS

Near the end of his life, Moses foretold the coming of someone else. He said, "The Lord your God will raise up for you a prophet like me from among you, from your countrymen, you shall listen to him" (Deuteronomy 18:15).

This was a prophecy about Jesus. Like Moses, Jesus would establish a new covenant between God and His people. The covenant of Moses was based on the law. It outlined commandments God gave Israel to govern their behaviour. The covenant of Jesus was based on grace, the unmerited favour and forgiveness of our Father in heaven.

Like Moses, Jesus would stand in the gap—not only for a single nation but also for the entire world. He would "turn away God's wrath from destroying them."[1] Jesus would fill the breach that sin had left between us and God and provide a path back to our Father.

The Bible tells us He loved the world so much that He was willing to sacrifice Himself to restore us in relationship with God. He tied His future to ours.

We didn't ask for this. We were Jesus' enemies. Yet, a restored connection was so important to Him that He died for us. We may have been His foes, but He was our friend.

Let's look to Jesus again as He hangs on the cross—skin hanging off His back, slowly suffocating, dying a torturous death at the hands of experts in torture—for us. He went through unimaginable suffering. No sacrifice was beyond His love.

Sometimes, we expect love to be clean, attractive, fairy tale-like.

God's love isn't like that. It's pure, but not clean. It gets dirty, sweaty, smelly, gross. It gets bloody, beaten, bruised, and ugly. It pushes the limits and will not settle for anything less than its object.

God's love is scary, because it's untamed, passionate, and willing to rip itself apart, limb from limb. It is ferocious, untiring, and unyielding. And it is perfect.

Paul

Saul hated Jesus and the blasphemous cult that polluted the Jewish religion. He poured all his time and energy into eradicating Christ-followers. He hunted them down. He threw them in prison. He cast his vote against them in capital cases and cheered their deaths.

He was wrong.

He discovered this one day while on special deployment to destroy more Christians. Jesus met him on the road to Damascus. Both Saul's name and heart changed that day. He went blind, but never had he seen more clearly.[2]

After he was healed by a brave man named Ananias, Paul poured everything into proclaiming Jesus as Messiah. The same energy that had destroyed Christians was now used to develop new believers. For his efforts, Paul was persecuted. Here's a partial list, taken from 2 Corinthians 11, of what he endured:

- Multiple times: thrown in prison
- Multiple times: flogged
- Many times: exposed to death

- Five times: received thirty-nine lashes (this would kill most people)
- Three times: beaten with rods
- Once: stoned (being pelted with rocks was a common form of capital punishment)
- Three times: shipwrecked
- Once spent a night floating around on the open sea
- Constantly on the move, running for his life
- Often without sleep, hungry, thirsty, cold, naked

Paul's efforts to spread Jesus' good news reached not only the Jewish people but also the gentiles. In his letter to the Romans, he proclaimed a fervent love for his people. Distressed that more were not turning to Jesus, he wrote:

> I am telling the truth in Christ, I am not lying, my conscience testifies with me in the Holy Spirit, that I have great sorrow and unceasing grief in my heart. For I could wish that I myself were accursed, separated from Christ for the sake of my brethren, my kinsmen according to the flesh, who are Israelites, to whom belongs the adoption as sons, and the glory and the covenants and the giving of the Law and the temple service and the promises, whose are the fathers, and from whom is the Christ according to the flesh, who is over all, God blessed forever. Amen.
>
> ROMANS 9:1–5

Keep in mind: for the most part, the Jews hated Paul. They sabotaged his ministry, plotted his capture, and tried to murder him on numerous occasions.

Paul forgave them. He loved them. He wanted to do whatever it took to draw them to Christ. He was prepared to give up his own future so they could have one.

Perhaps by now you're starting to see the theme running through these people's lives. They exhibited forgiveness towards those who had been their enemies. Their love was so great they were willing to link their futures with their adversaries'.

A decision to stand in the gap for our foes cannot be forced. Above all, it must be born of genuine, supernatural love flowing from the deepest desires of our hearts. If we pressure ourselves, we wrong ourselves. Doing so undermines our future ability to heal. The consequences can be dire when our bodies and psyches react. We must not victimize ourselves. If, like the prophet Ezekiel, we choose not to stand in the gap for our enemies, God will not condemn us. He won't question why we haven't done so. No dark mark will be struck against our names.

Standing in the gap is more than simple obedience. It puts 'self' on the line. It goes all in. There can be nothing artificial about it. God is not fooled by outward showmanship.

He knows our inner being. We can hide nothing from Him. Without complete authenticity, false attempts at standing in the gap are sin. If we try this without God's enablement, we fraudulently claim a supernatural miracle in our hearts. We're striving to be 'super-Christians', when this is not asked of us. This demonstrates a pride that elicits God's judgment—not on our enemies but on ourselves.

We are not the saviour of the world. Jesus is. If we try to stand in the gap based on some sort of misplaced saviour complex, we set ourselves up as false gods. And God destroys idols. Remember, this is a dangerous side of forgiveness. We must not treat it with anything less than soul-searching humility and honesty.

There's no shame in not standing in the gap for our enemies, and there's no pride if we have done so. All that exists is gratitude for God's forgiveness and for that blessed time when Jesus stood in the gap for us.

23

Better Than Before

> *Man's ruin was so terrible, and so profound that there was but one alternative open to the Eternal God. Either He must sweep out and destroy utterly the race, or else in infinite patience, and through long processes, lead it back to Himself. He chose the pathway of reconciliation in His infinite grace, at what cost the story of Christ alone perfectly reveals.*
>
> G. CAMPBELL MORGAN, BRITISH EVANGELIST, PREACHER

EVERYTHING WE'VE DISCUSSED UNTIL NOW can be accomplished one on one with God without the participation of the one who has hurt us.

This is not the case with reconciliation. To be successful, both parties must undergo a heart change. Sometimes, relational restoration isn't possible. If you have a desire for it but the other person does not, you may not be able to go beyond forgiving them. The wounding party must be willing to admit responsibility for his or her actions, adjust, and not expect a restored relationship without putting in work. After all, "the way to reconciliation lies through an effective grappling with the root cause of the enmity."[1]

We can approach this topic from a godly and obedient mindset only when we cultivate a deep reliance on our heavenly Father. When we submit ourselves to Jesus and listen to

Him, He gives us the courage to obey. A God-honouring perspective will ultimately maximize emotional and spiritual health.

Relational reconciliation is close to the heart of God. Biblical history contains bounteous examples of the lengths He would go to in drawing us back to Himself. Reconciliation is the ideal of forgiveness—that is, forgiveness will often lead to a desire for restored relationship. When we forgive people, God enables us to pray earnestly for them. Our hearts open to the possibility of future harmony.

That said, each circumstance is unique. Restoration is not always wise or healthy. It's prudent to solicit the advice of a qualified Christian therapist, such as a registered psychotherapist, psychologist, or psychiatrist. Licensed professionals can be crucial in mitigating harmful situations and events. They can holistically address your specific circumstances and needs, and assist you in deciding what's healthiest.

Especially in the case of formerly abusive relationships, I would implore you to seek specialized help. A trained therapist will give targeted advice and will be well-versed in legal matters, mental health issues, sources of social support, and more. It's never a good idea to explore reconciliation with an abuser without the wise counsel of a professional. Total restoration is often not advisable for those who have suffered violent abuse.

This side of heaven, restoration is of course impossible if someone has passed away. Yet, this does not bar us from experiencing the freedom that forgiveness brings. We may achieve a sense of closure through a graveside visit. Reading Scripture there, praying, and talking to the imaginary person may help us lay down the former conflict and bitterness and allow our heavenly Father to guide us into an abundant and joyful future.

For now, let's return to considering non-abusive relationships with people who are still alive. It's important to gauge whether the other person has changed before fully investing ourselves. Some hurtful people may never recognize or admit they have sinned against us. This does not preclude forgiveness, but it may prevent reconciliation. We should prayerfully consider these words of Jesus: "Do not give what is holy to dogs, and do not throw your pearls before swine, or they will trample them under their feet, and turn and tear you to pieces" (Matthew 7:6).

Let's examine this passage in more detail.

Q: What are my pearls?

A: In the context of reconciliation, our 'pearls' are things that are precious to us and God. They are our desire for relational harmony in the wake of forgiveness.

Q: What are the swine?

A: In this case, 'swine' are people who do not value our pearls. We may initially feel that anyone who hurts us falls into the 'swine' category. However, this is not true. Some people may not have intended to hurt us and may be horrified to know the cost of their actions. Others may repent of their sins. They may still treasure their relationship with us. Such people would cherish the forgiveness and reconciliation we extend.

Q: What does it mean that the swine will trample my pearls under their feet?
A: In this metaphor, the swine don't care about the priceless treasures we offer them. Instead, they treat them with disdain, reject them, and destroy them. There is no gratitude, no humility. There is only wanton destruction.

Q: What does it mean that the swine will then turn and tear me to pieces?
A: When our enemies' contempt reaches critical mass, evil multiplies. Swine are not content with only destroying things that are precious to us. They want to demolish us as well. This may stem from a guilty conscience and the conclusion that the only way to remove their discomfort is to annihilate the one who has caused it. They may be proud and not want to admit they are wrong. Whatever the reason, it can be perilous to offer an unrepentant person the jewel of reconciliation.

Remember the story of Joseph in the Old Testament? Before he and his brothers reconciled, Joseph made sure they had changed. He ascertained that his pearl would be valued and appreciated. He verified that his brothers weren't swine who would once more act to destroy him.

For Joseph, forgiveness would have let his brothers buy food and go their way without making himself known. Reconciliation invited them to live near him in Egypt.

If those who have injured us are unrepentant, then following Jesus' directive, we should forgo reconciliation for now. We should be willing to lead joyful and complete lives without the person who has wronged us. We entrust our desires for restoration to God, and in faith we leave them at the foot of Jesus' cross. Perhaps He will grant our hearts' desire later, but for now, we should choose to cultivate lives of spiritual and emotional health.

Our gratitude to God enables us to savour the abundant life Jesus promised and doesn't allow destructive people to steal our joy. Jesus paid for victory with His precious blood and has generously imparted it to us. We do well to not live burdened by regret over a relationship another person has chosen to discard. It's far better to adopt an attitude of thankfulness for the things we do have and for the wonderful future our Father has planned for us.

The reconciliation process may differ according to the people and situations involved, though a few attributes are common in most cases. At first, we may not know for certain that all the requisite elements for relational healing are present. If we've been hurt but not abused, we may choose to dip our toes into the water of reconciliation to gauge its temperature.

If restoration is to be possible, one party will have to make a move amid uncertainty and hope to find these elements present.

1. Both parties have a strong desire for repaired relationship.

Without a hunger and commitment to work towards reconciliation, it is unattainable. This process is hard! If we lack the resolve to keep going, our efforts are unlikely to succeed.

2. The wounded party forgives the person who has hurt him or her.

Without forgiveness, healthy reconciliation is impossible. Any attempt will only result in toxicity as bitterness grows in the heart of the wounded. Resentment eventually works itself out in destructive actions towards the guilty party. In time, it damages the hurt person too. We cannot fake forgiveness. It has to be genuine. A lack of forgiveness will always be exposed over the long term, usually in devastating ways.

3. The individual who has caused the wounds is willing to admit mistakes or sin.

This can be difficult to hear, but sometimes our injuries are not the result of sin. From time to time they're created by mistake. Whether hurt stems from sin or mistakes, a wounded person often needs to hear some sort of regret expressed—one that does not place blame on him or her.

Dr. Les Greenberg, from York University in Toronto, has conducted studies on forgiveness that show true reconciliation and healing are possible only when the injured party is sure the antagonist understands the hurt and regrets the actions that caused it.[2]

4. *The wounding party is willing to be forgiven.*

If the offender is unwilling to be forgiven, he or she may commit some type of self-sabotage. This can be destructive to everyone involved, so if this is the case, it would be better to delay attempts at reconciliation.

Sometimes, it may be possible to help the wounding party forgive him or herself.[3] However, a hurt person isn't always able to engage in this way, and such an action should not be forced. An introduction to someone else who can aid in self-forgiveness may be in order.

5. *Both parties are willing to work at restoring trust.*

This process is long and time-consuming. Sometimes, additional issues surface. They may require additional forgiveness.

As with any type of healing, the path to reconciliation is not always linear. A good day may be followed by a bad one, when there seems to be backsliding. Don't despair! These fluctuations are a natural part of the healing cycle. Continually entrust yourself to Jesus in those times. Remember: "God, who began a good work within you, will continue His work until it is finally finished on the day when Christ Jesus returns" (Philippians 1:6, NLT). Patience is key in allowing our Saviour to protect and restore our hearts.

In North America, we embrace the concept of boundaries. For instance, my feelings are my own. Yours are not mine. I'm responsible for my feelings and the actions stemming from them. I'm not accountable for your actions or feelings.[4]

If I try to take ownership of your emotions and conduct, I diminish you as a person; somehow, I'm better than you because I'm responsible not only for myself but also for you. For example, my mindset may imply, *You can't handle your own emotions or deeds, so let me take them from you. I've got it.* This mentality makes you into a lesser person than I.

By contrast, a healthy attitude says, "What's mine is mine, and what's yours is yours." We can have an emotionally healthy relationship when we both take responsibility for ourselves.

Though this is true, in our highly individualistic culture we sometimes take these concepts too far. We may not be responsible *for* each other, but we are responsible *to* each other.[5] We're answerable for the hurts we cause. We're compelled by love to "bear one another's burdens" (Galatians 6:2, ESV), as the apostle Paul said. This includes helping each other in spiritual struggles.

We may agree with the idea that we're responsible to our fellow human beings if we've caused hurt. But what about a

Christian brother or sister who is jealous of us through no fault of our own? After all, jealousy is a feeling. We can't be bound by another person's emotions. A typical solution, when confronted with such one-sided conflict, is to shrug and say, "That's your problem" and walk away.

Living in Japan, a community-focussed culture, I've learnt that we in the West may take less responsibility for reconciliation than perhaps we should. Even in the case of jealousy, there are times when we shouldn't just slip away. Sometimes we're still responsible *to* our Christian brothers and sisters.

When this thought first crossed my mind one night in the dark before the dawn, my psyche reared back in indignation.

"Am I my brother's keeper?" I said along with Cain who, incidentally, killed his brother.

"Yes," God said to both of us.

I remembered Jesus' words: "But I say to you who hear, love your enemies, do good to those who hate you, bless those who curse you, pray for those who mistreat you" (Luke 6:27–28).

That night, I realized the principle behind the message. When other people have a problem with us, whether or not it's our fault, we still have a responsibility to them. We have an obligation to help resolve their antagonistic feelings so we can live together in peace. We have a duty to bear this burden with them.

As Jesus said, "Therefore if you are presenting your offering at the altar, and there remember that your brother has something against you, leave your offering there before the altar and go; first be reconciled to your brother, and then come and present your offering" (Matthew 5:23).

Christians often misquote or misunderstand this Scripture. Notice it says, "if your brother has something against you", not "if you have something against your brother". If there's trouble in our brothers' or sisters' hearts, we are not off the hook.

This passage doesn't specify whether there has been wrongdoing. It doesn't matter if the offense is in our brother's mind or in our own deeds. Either way, we're responsible to our brother to go and be reconciled.

I once experienced a major snub at the hands of a fellow Christian whom I'll call Sherry. She's Japanese. I thought for a while that I would just absorb the hurt, forgive, and move on, hoping her harshness was unintended. If the problem cropped up again, I would deal with it then.

Soon after this, I had my epiphany about being responsible to our brothers and sisters in times of conflict, even if we've done nothing wrong. In this case, I had no idea if I'd made a cultural faux pas or if Sherry's actions stemmed from something internal. I recognized, however, that it was my responsibility to either make amends or help her move past her inner struggle by doing things to soften her heart towards me.

I didn't know enough Japanese to inject subtlety or nuance into my communication. So, I thought I would approach the friction head-on, begging forgiveness for my method. When I went to talk with her, though, I felt muzzled. I couldn't seem to start the conversation. At first, I wondered if this stemmed from my discomfort with using a style of direct conflict resolution, but later realized perhaps God was preventing me from making a mistake.

I considered a more circuitous route. I went out of my way to spend time with Sherry. Perhaps if I were really loving towards her, this would soften her heart. If I spent time with her, some unforeseen opportunity might present itself.

It did.

During a church fellowship time, she started playing a rhythmic game with her young daughter.

"Wow! I couldn't do that!" Time for a big dose of vulnerability. I related several comical tales of my incompetence at rhythmic pursuits. By the end, she was in stitches.

"So, you see," I said, "I'm always impressed whenever someone does what you just did. I'd love to be able to do that, but I don't think it's possible."

The fellowship time continued. Less than five minutes later, she sidled up and told me a secret she had been keeping. This secret partially explained her previous behaviour, and her sharing resolved the snub. I could react in affirmation and tell her—in a socially acceptable, indirect way, of course!—how much I loved her. The relationship was restored, or rather, improved. I was now one of the trusted few to know her secret.

We can apply several principles from this experience to other one-sided conflicts.

1. We are our brothers' keepers. Though we're not responsible *for* each other's feelings, we are responsible *to* our fellow Christians.

2. We should be open to sharing one another's burdens, particularly when dealing with spiritual struggles.

3. We ought to walk toward, rather than away from, our brothers and sisters when they encounter internal or one-sided conflict. We have a responsibility to love and spend time with them. We can't afford to leave them alone when they're struggling, even if we have done nothing wrong. This doesn't mean we annoy them until they pay lip service to reconciliation; it does mean we go above and beyond to find little ways of pouring blessing into their lives in a humble, unobtrusive manner.

4. Here are some ways to help our Christian brothers and sisters be victorious over inner conflict:

    - Pray for them. Ask God to guide you. He knows their hearts better than you and even better than they do.

- Spend time with them. Find ways to show love—not on your terms but on theirs. Sometimes the things we think are caring are not perceived that way by other people. As long as it's not sinful, adapt to what they consider loving.
- Don't indulge your pride. Don't brag. Don't allow yourself to feel superior because you're not struggling. Your turn will come!
- Be vulnerable. Share about your own inadequacies.
- Find something to like and praise about them. Tell them what you admire and why. Make sure you're genuine. If you can't think of something right away, be patient, keep your eyes open, and pray for enlightenment. Don't just make something up; people can smell a fake. Tell them you want to be like them in a good character trait or a certain ability. If they know this, it may help bring balance to your relationship; perhaps they've been wanting to be like you!

If we're honest with ourselves, sometimes it can feel nice when someone is jealous of us. We have something that someone else wants. We're superior. *Their* jealousy feeds *our* pride.

Yet, the apostle Paul said, "Let us not judge one another anymore, but rather determine this—not to put an obstacle or a stumbling block in a brother's way" (Romans 14:13).

The truth is there is no room for one-upmanship in the Christian life. When Paul talked about running the race, he didn't have competition in mind. We're not supposed to focus on coming in first place. We're meant to help one another across the finish line. Today, it may be our job to lend a hand to someone else. But tomorrow that same person may help us!

Further examples of reconciliation

While on furlough, Peter and I once encountered relational conflict with another Christian couple. We'll call them Ophelia and Orlando Overhill. It happened right at the end of our time in Canada. We tried to resolve the discord over the telephone before departing, but it only got worse. Our departure was set, and we had no time to mend the relationship in person before we left. We tried to comfort ourselves with the idea that our lives don't normally intersect with those of the Overhills. If the relationship was irreparable, we wouldn't have to be reminded of it much. However, Peter and I vowed that the next time we were in Canada, we would prioritize meeting with the Overhills in the hope we might still mend our bond.

Over the following months of ministry in Japan, the Overhills were often in my mind and heart. I prayed over our rift in devotions almost every day. God taught us many things about reconciliation that year. By the end, we were no longer content with waiting until our return to Canada to mend things. We needed to try sooner.

We pumped a lot of prayer into preparing for that meeting. We could now see we had made several mistakes in the relationship too. In our conversation, we decided not to dwell on the things we'd suffered and instead focus on the ways they had. If explanations were needed, we would offer them only to help them forgive us, not to justify or defend ourselves.

Preparation complete, hands and knees trembling, we made the phone call.

Following the initial pleasantries, I said, "We're brothers and sisters in Jesus' family. Over the past year, we've been thinking a lot about what happened between us and praying for you almost every day. We've realized it's unacceptable to leave things as they are. This is not the sort of relationship God has called us to have with each other. If you're willing, let's try to reconcile."

Orlando sighed deeply.

"What do you want me to apologize for?"

Peter and I were shocked into speechlessness. Orlando, a former pastor, understood 'reconciliation' to be a demand for apology.

"No," we said. "We're the ones who want to apologize to you!"

What followed was a delightful conversation that not only corrected misconceptions on both sides but also resulted in deepened respect for each other.

In university, I had a friend I'll call Jacob. He wasn't a Christian. Peter and I often spent time with him following graduation.

Shortly after Peter and I left for Japan, I had a falling out with Jacob. I hadn't paid as much attention as I should have to the way I chose my words in our correspondence. Jacob took issue with that. Despite my best efforts to restore relational equilibrium, the exchange ended with his request that I never contact him again.

Until then, I had never experienced this kind of end to a friendship. It left me startled and confused. I honoured his desire for six years, but finally I could no longer ignore my discontent with the fracture in our relationship.

In my earlier days, I'd thought I understood how other Canadians may react to certain stimuli. With maturity, I understood my lack of knowledge a little better. I'd been learning loads about how Eastern cultures communicate; these methods are often the polar opposite of how Westerners express themselves. I realized that even though Jacob was born in Canada, several Eastern communication principles might apply to him, given his family's still-strong ties with that part of the world. I examined my former actions through the lens of those insights.

I recognized that Jacob's parting shot, ascribing several negative attributes to my character, was not as far off base as I had originally thought. The attitudes and behaviours I'd chalked up to youthful ignorance could have appeared arrogant, for example. His perceptions were no less valid than mine. The more I considered what had happened, the more I wanted to apologize.

I sent him an email. He could ignore it if he wanted. Although my message wasn't quite as stark as the list below, the content was pretty simple:

1. An apology for breaking the communication embargo he'd requested and a promise to return to radio silence indefinitely after this.
2. "You were right."
3. "I'm sorry."
4. The hope that my message might ease any emotional burdens I might have caused by my former behaviour.

To my surprise, Jacob responded right away. He had been battling a few personal demons during the original conflict and had no memory of our falling out. He forgave my inadequacies, and we resumed our warm relationship; eventually, he would ask Peter and me to tutor him in studying the Bible!

You might have noticed by now that seeking reconciliation is not the same as seeking an apology. In these examples, it was necessary for me to forgive my adversaries before contacting them. I only wanted to apologize *to* them by the time of contact.

When we forgive, we're given eyes to see that God deeply loves all people, including our foes. Since we love God, we extend that same love to the people we've forgiven. As one police officer would discover, love pursues and so does a desire for reconciliation.

A man we'll call Patrick McDunn was on a routine police patrol in the summer of 1986. On the lookout following a string of petty crimes near Central Park in New York City, he and his partner came across three teenagers. The five had just begun to talk together when one boy pulled out a gun and shot Patrick three times.[6]

At first, the doctors thought he wouldn't make it. One gunshot had been to his head and another to his throat—that bullet lodged in his spine. Patrick went from leading an active lifestyle to being paralyzed and needing a ventilator to breathe. He could no longer wait on his new, pregnant wife but required care himself, for even the most basic tasks.

Following his son's birth, Patrick realized he didn't want to be ruled by bitterness and hatred anymore. He had a different life now, and he wanted his heart to be different too. He chose to forgive.

He wrote letters to his attacker. He received no response at first. Eventually the young man, whom we'll call Shawn, wrote back. The two became friends. Following years of correspondence, Shawn called Patrick and his family one night with an apology. They accepted it.

A few days after Shawn was released from prison, he died in a motorcycle accident. Patrick and Shawn never got the chance to meet again in person.

When asked about his experience, Patrick says, "I forgave Shawn because I believe the only thing worse than receiving a bullet in my spine would have been to nurture revenge in my heart. Such an attitude would have extended my injury to my soul, hurting my wife, son, and others even more. It's bad enough that the physical effects are permanent, but at least I can choose to prevent spiritual injury.

"Of course I didn't forgive Shawn right away. It took time. Things have evolved over fourteen years. I think about it almost every day. But I can say this: I've never regretted forgiving him."[7]

God enabled Patrick to forgive Shawn. Through that forgiveness came an undeniable desire for reconciliation. When Patrick tirelessly pursued a relationship, Shawn's heart was changed, and friendship was possible. We may never know how this affected Shawn's life. But of one thing we can be sure—it had an impact.

Forgiveness always does.

Closing Part VI

Food for Thought

LIVING TRAPPED IN UNFORGIVENESS DRAINS our emotional energy, our physical stamina, our creativity, and our spiritual potential for godliness. Yet if we decide to forgive, we honour God and the people He created us to be. Many of the things we learn will be transferrable to other aspects of our lives and may enable us to facilitate healing in others. A decision to forgive is one to embark on a journey of intensive learning and healing, and unleash our potential to become the people we've always wanted to be.

The struggle you and I experience along the way to forgiveness is not wasted. Jesus is with us through every spasm of heart, through every bit of effort, through every wound prodded. He understands the cost. And He is suffering with us. He catches each of our tears in His bottle. They are precious to Him. These sacrifices—and well He knows they *are* sacrifices!—are the truest form of worship we can offer our beloved King.

When we request His help, He tenderly bends to our aid. And when our gargantuan efforts are complete, when we're able to say the words "I forgive you", Jesus slowly smiles.

"Well done, good and faithful servant," He whispers. "Now enter into My joy." (Matthew 25:21, my paraphrase) And we do.

Going Deeper

1. What do you think when you hear we're not to take vengeance on our enemies? How do you feel?

2. Fyodor Dostoyevsky once wrote, "Love in action is a harsh and dreadful thing compared with love in dreams. Love in dreams is greedy for immediate action, rapidly performed and in sight of all. Men will even give their lives if only the ordeal does not last long but is soon over, with all looking on and applauding. But active love is labor and fortitude."[1]

   Make a list of ways that God's love is mighty like this. How may you also love God and others mightily?

3. Share a story of a time when you were able to reconcile with someone following a conflict. If you don't have an

experience like this, think through conflicts you've experienced in the past. Is there someone you can make peace with? Is there someone you need to forgive?

4. Forgiveness frees our minds and spirits from the clutter and distraction of bitterness. With it gone, how will you 'redecorate' your mind and life? What will you do with your extra emotional, spiritual, and physical energy?

Notes

For full bibliographic information on these entries, see the Bibliography section at the end.

Chapter 1: Keeping Holy in a Clash
1. Marion Goertz, email message to author, May 12, 2015.
2. In this study, respondents were asked if they identified with a particular faith group. There was no measure of personal commitment to stated beliefs.
3. George Barna, *The Second Coming of the Church*, 20–24 of 267 in e-book.
4. Frank Thielman, *The NIV Application Commentary: Philippians*, Philippians 4:5 entry.
5. *NASB Strong's Bible Text*, Philippians 4:5 entry.
6. See chapter 17 for a guide on how to do this.

Chapter 4: Which Fruit?
1. Dr. Leon F. Seltzer, "Don't Let Your Anger 'Mature' Into Bitterness," *Psychology Today*.
2. Dr. Rick Nauert, "Bitterness can make you sick," *PsychCentral*.

Closing Part I
1. David Augsburger, *The New Freedom of Forgiveness*, 21 of 216 in e-book.

Part II: Understanding Forgiveness
1. Tara John, "JK Rowling Reveals Why Harry Potter Named His Son After Professor Snape," *Time*.

Chapter 5: What Forgiveness Isn't
1. See Dr. Leon F. Seltzer, "Trust Your Feelings?…Maybe Not," *Psychology Today*; and Dr. Gillian McCann and Gitte Bechsgaard, "Don't Trust Your Feelings!" *Psychology Today*.
2. The place where the moneychangers had set up their tables was designated as the only place where foreigners were allowed to come and pray at the temple.

(For more on this, see Leon Morris, *Pillar New Testament Commentary: The Gospel According to Matthew*, Matthew 21:12–13 entries.)

3. By the world's view, humans are the standard for all judgment of right and wrong. In North America, though our legal system was originally based on biblical principles, now it's based on precedent—past decisions made by humans, which we assume are correct. The fact that our precedents no longer match biblical principles is not surprising. The sin in each of us naturally diverges from following God. Our reliance on precedent can yield a shaky foundation for future decision-making. After all, human decisions can be prone to error. Basing our future on the assumption that all previous decisions have been correct is risky at best.
4. Bill Bright, *Have You Made the Wonderful Discovery of the Spirit-Filled Life?*, 13.
5. Henry Drummond, *The Greatest Thing in All the World and Other Addresses*, 21.
6. Dr. Susan Krauss Whitbourne, "5 Ways to Get Your Unwanted Emotions Under Control," *Psychology Today*.
7. *The Canadian Oxford Dictionary*, 697.
8. Despite my best efforts, I've been unable to track down the original source and wording for this idea.
9. Martin Luther King Jr., *Strength to Love*, 95 of 271 in e-book.
10. Johann Christoph Arnold, *Why Forgive?*, 167.
11. Warren W. Wiersbe, *The Bible Exposition Commentary*, 1.244.
12. Johann Christoph Arnold, *Why Forgive?*, 71.

Chapter 6: What Forgiveness Is

1. "Forgive", dictionary.com.
2. Here are two examples. (1) We've been told that before Christianity came to Japan, the Japanese word for "love" only referred to sexual love. (2) In Japan, trust is the foundation for all relationships; it often takes many years, even decades, for deep friendships to form. Mutual indebtedness, built by exchanging gifts and favours, is a key ingredient for relational trust. In Japan, there exists an emotion that we don't experience in our native North American

culture. It's called *amae*. It's the feeling of pleasure that a Japanese person experiences when someone else asks for a favour. That's because, in asking for something, the requester has specifically chosen to deepen a relationship with the recipient of the request. This yields a special kind of relational joy that we don't experience in the West.
3. Eugene E. Carpenter and Philip W. Comfort, *Holman Treasury of Key Bible Words: 200 Greek and 200 Hebrew Words Defined and Explained*, 64.
4. Ibid, 284.
5. Ibid.

CHAPTER 7: HOW FORGIVENESS CHANGED THE WORLD
1. Alvin J. Schmidt, *How Christianity Changed the World*.
2. Details of this story have been taken from Elisabeth Elliot, *Through Gates of Splendor*.
3. Personal conversation with Dave and Joyce Findlay, who know the family of Nate Saint, 2016.
4. Elisabeth Elliot, *Through Gates of Splendor*, forward section.
5. Marshall Frady, *Martin Luther King Jr.: A Life*, 79 of 355 in e-book.
6. Details of this story taken from Philip Yancey, *Soul Survivor*, 26–85 of 627 in e-book; and from Marshall Frady, *Martin Luther King Jr.: A Life*.
7. Philip Yancey, *Soul Survivor*, 59 of 627 in e-book.
8. Martin Luther King Jr., *Strength to Love*, 85 of 271 in e-book.
9. Details of this story taken from Corrie ten Boom, *The Hiding Place*.
10. Corrie ten Boom, *The Hiding Place*, 458 of 499 in e-book.

CHAPTER 8: HOW FORGIVENESS CHANGES THE WORLD FOR US
1. Details of this story taken from Johann Christoph Arnold, *Why Forgive?*, 80–85.
2. Johann Christoph Arnold, *Why Forgive?*, 85.
3. Details of this story taken from Johann Christoph Arnold, *Why Forgive?*, 208–209.
4. John Holusha, "Students Killed by Gunman at Amish Schoolhouse", *The New York Times*.

5. Ibid.
6. "Text of Roberts' Suicide Note", AP News.
7. Johann Christoph Arnold, *Why Forgive?*, 208–209.
8. Details of this story taken from Johann Christoph Arnold, *Why Forgive?*, 195–202.
9. Johann Christoph Arnold, *Why Forgive?*, 195–202.
10. Ibid, 200.
11. Details of this story taken from Johann Christoph Arnold, *Why Forgive?*, 10–11.
12. Johann Christoph Arnold, *Why Forgive?*, 11.

Closing Part II
1. Corrie ten Boom, *The Hiding Place*, 459 of 499 in e-book.
2. Commentary source unknown.

Part III: Our Foundation
1. Kathy W. Ross and Rosemary Stacy, "John Wesley and Savannah."
2. R. Kent Hughes, *The Sermon on the Mount: The Message of the Kingdom*, 189.

Chapter 9: Who We Are
1. Duane Elmer, *Cross-Cultural Conflict*, 25.
2. Greg Boyd, "One Church #1: Baptist to Anabaptist," minute 24.

Chapter 10: The Importance of Forgiveness
1. Douglas Stuart, "Lecture 4: Out of Egypt and Into the Promise," Old Testament Survey I: Creation, Covenant, & Kings.
2. I.D.E. Thomas, *The Golden Treasury of Puritan Quotations*, 111.
3. My paraphrase, Charles Haddon Spurgeon, *Metropolitan Tabernacle Pulpit*.

Chapter 11: Forgiveness Belongs to Our God
1. Alexander Pope, "An Essay on Criticism," as quoted in *The Merriam-Webster Dictionary of Quotations*, 519; and Eugene E. Carpenter and Philip W. Comfort, Holman *Treasury of Key Bible Words: 200 Greek and 200 Hebrew Words Defined and Explained*, 284.

Chapter 12: BC and AD

1. In a handful of cases, someone living in Old Testament times refused to forgive, or asked God not to forgive, a third party.
2. There is only one instance when the Bible says forgiveness will not be given. That is when people commit the unforgivable sin of blaspheming against the Holy Spirit (Mark 3:29).
3. There are also several mentions of the blood of murder victims having been avenged.
4. One of the two outlier verses talks about the government being the avenger of wrongdoing. The last retells the Old Testament story of Moses avenging an oppressed Hebrew slave who was wronged by an Egyptian.

Closing Part III

1. (sic) Hamilton Nolan, "A Letter from Ray Jasper, Who Is About to be Executed," *Gawker*.
2. Forgiveness—A Matter of Life and Death for Christians", Bible Truths Revealed.

Part IV: Freedom in Forgiveness

1. Stephen Liggins, "What We Can Learn from African Christians," *The Briefing*.
2. Shusaku Endo, *Silence*, p ix–x.

Chapter 13: How God Forgives Us

1. Andrew Peterson, "Just as I Am," track 5 on *Love & Thunder*. Copyright © 2003 New Spring Publishing Inc. (ASCAP) (adm. at CapitolCMGPublishing.com). All rights reserved. Used by permission.
2. Ibid.
3. Brennan Manning, *Ruthless Trust: The Ragamuffin's Path to God*, 189 of 300 in e-book.
4. Beth Moore, *When Godly People Do Ungodly Things*, 124–125 of 437 in ebook.
5. Paraphrase of C. H. Spurgeon, *Spurgeon on Prayer & Spiritual Warfare*, 501 of 576 in e-book.

Chapter 14: Selling Our Birthright

1. I first came across this idea through Max Lucado (as quoted on "Forgiveness Opens the Door for Change!", *Living More Abundantly*) but Lewis Smedes (*Forgive and Forget*, 133) wrote about it earlier, and there may have been others earlier still.
2. Remember, a deferred decision is itself a decision.

Chapter 15: Willing Victims?

1. R. Francis Hingley, "Joseph Stalin," Encyclopedia Britannica.
2. Simon Sebag Montefiore, *Young Stalin*, 29.
3. Ibid, 30–31.
4. Francois Murphy, "Hitler's older brother was in fact younger and died early, historian says," Reuters.
5. D.J.R. Bruckner, "The Stage: Hitler's Childhood," *The New York Times*.
6. Ian Kershaw, *Hitler: A Biography*, 14.
7. Nikolay Andreyev, "Ivan the Terrible," *Encyclopedia Britannica*; and D. Lieven, et. al., "Russia," *Encyclopedia Britannica*.
8. Ibid.
9. B.P. Perry, "Why Was Ivan so Terrible?" *History*.
10. *The British Cyclopaedia of the Arts, Science, History, Geography, Literature, Natural History, and Biography*, 1838.
11. Robert Payne and Nikita Romanoff, *Ivan the Terrible*, 282.
12. Nikolay Andreyev, "Ivan the Terrible," *Encyclopedia Britannica*; and D. Lieven, et. al., "Russia," *Encyclopedia Britannica*.

Closing Part IV

1. Details of this story have been taken from Johann Christoph Arnold, *Why Forgive?*, 24–30.
2. Johann Christoph Arnold, *Why Forgive?*, 24.
3. Ibid 29.

Chapter 16: Shaping our Attitudes

1. Morgan Housel, "6 Important Lessons from Nobel-Prize Winning Psychologist Daniel Kahneman," *Business Insider*.

2. Fyodor Dostoyevsky, *The Brothers Karamazov*, 758–760 of 811 in e-book.
3. Beth Moore, *When Godly People Do Ungodly Things*, 189 of 437 in e-book.
4. There is a third type of sin—a hybrid. It starts out as wilful and eventually becomes hidden. When we sin and choose to ignore the Holy Spirit's conviction, we dull our consciences. The Bible talks about this as "quenching the Holy Spirit" (1 Thessalonians 5:19). In doing so, we lose the ability to discern what is sin and what is not. Our iniquity becomes hidden from us and we may continue without feeling guilty (see Beth Moore, *When Godly People Do Ungodly Things*, 189). With ineffective consciences, we become capable of carrying out horrific wrongdoing.
5. *Olive Tree Enhanced Strong's Dictionary*, h7686.
6. R. Kent Hughes, *The Sermon on the Mount: The Message of the Kingdom*, 49.
7. See Beth Moore, *When Godly People Do Ungodly Things*, 155 of 437 in e-book.

CHAPTER 17: FORGIVENESS IN PRACTICE

1. Norman Doidge, *The Brain That Changes Itself*, 355–356 of 662 in e-book.
2. Ibid, 350 of 662 in e-book.
3. Terry C. Muck, *Sins of the Body: Ministry in a Sexual Society*, 196–197.
4. Roger Campbell, "The Unmerciful Servant," in *Preach for a Year #2*, 184.
5. Karen Andersen, "Tea and Christianity," *Crisis Magazine*. Despite my best efforts, I was not able to fully corroborate this information with an independent source. However, I was able to corroborate the following: (1) Japanese Christians were known to hide in plain sight during this time of persecution, (2) the tea ceremony closely resembles communion, and (3) Japanese Christians were known to sometimes meet in tea houses.
6. Johann Christoph Arnold, *Why Forgive?*, 1.
7. Preston, Gary D., *Character Forged from Conflict: Staying Connected to God During Controversy*, 67–69.
8. Ibid, 69–73.

CHAPTER 19: TESTING OUR FORGIVENESS

1. All but the first question in this list are taken from David Seamands, *Healing for Damaged Emotions*, as quoted by Terry Muck, *When to Take a Risk: A Guide to Pastoral Decision-Making*.

2. Cole, Simone Weil, *A Modern Pilgrimage*, as quoted in Philip Yancy, *Soul Survivor*, 216 of 627 in e-book.

Chapter 20: Things That Make Forgiveness Harder

1. Since God has given us stewardship over our own bodies and spirits, we should carefully consider how to protect the things God has given us. We may need to extract ourselves from harmful situations, keeping in mind that hurt isn't always the same as harm (see Henry Cloud and John Townsend, *Boundaries*, 109 of 420 in e-book). Each circumstance is different. Dealing with a difficult work environment is different from dealing with a difficult marriage. We should seek out therapy and godly counsel in deciding what to do.
2. Deathbed joke (1856) attributed as last words of Heinrich Heine, as quoted in French by Sigmund Freud, *The Joke and Its Relation to the Unconscious*, 366–367 of 674 in e-book.
3. Oswald Chambers, *My Utmost for His Highest*, "November 20: The Forgiveness of God".

Closing Part V

1. Daniel F. Stone, "The fiery partnership between two great psychologists can help explain why some relationships fall apart," *Quartz*.

Chapter 21: Love Your Enemies

1. Peter Limmer, "The Sign of Jonah".
2. "Messiah," *The New Bible Dictionary*.
3. James R. Edwards, *Pillar New Testament Commentary: The Gospel According to Luke*, Luke 11:29–32 entry.
4. "Plunder," dictionary.com.
5. Martin Luther King Jr., *Strength to Love*, 80–88.
6. Bruxy Cavey, PowerPoint presentation emailed to the author, June 30, 2016.

Chapter 22: Standing in the Gap

1. This comes from a paraphrase of Psalm 106:23, a prayer of Moses referring to his own actions. Romans 3:23–26 shows us that on a larger scale Jesus was

the conduit by which God's wrath was diverted, thus allowing us to be made right with God.
2. Andrew Peterson, "The Chasing Song," recorded March 2000, track 2 on *Carried Along*, Brentwood Records, compact disc.

CHAPTER 23: BETTER THAN BEFORE

1. "Reconciliation," *The New Bible Dictionary*.
2. Adrienne Brown, "How to mend a family feud," *Canadian Living*.
3. Refer to chapter 18 for more information on self-forgiveness.
4. Henry Cloud and John Townsend, *Boundaries*, 29–34 of 276 in e-book.
5. Ibid, 22–23 of 276 in e-book.
6. Details of this story taken from Johann Christoph Arnold, *Why Forgive?*, 174–181.
7. Johann Christoph Arnold, *Why Forgive?*, 180.

CLOSING PART VI

1. Fyodor Dostoyevsky, *The Brothers Karamazov*, 55 of 811 in e-book.

Bibliography

"Forgive." Dictionary.com. Accessed 29 August 2019. https://www.dictionary.com/browse/forgive?s=t.

"Forgiveness—A Matter of Life or Death for Christians." Bible Truths Revealed. Last modified 28 July 2013. http://bible-truths-revealed.com/adv11.html.

"James Edward Oglethorpe." *Encyclopedia Britannica*. Last modified 18 December 2021. https://www.britannica.com/biography/James-Edward-Oglethorpe.

"John Wesley." *Encyclopedia Britannica*. Last modified 26 February 2022. https://www.britannica.com/biography/John-Wesley.

"Plunder." Dictionary.com. Accessed 3 September 2019. https://www.dictionary.com/browse/plunder?s=t.

"Text of Roberts' Suicide Note." AP News. Last modified 4 October 2006. https://apnews.com/article/825bbae73a2-c58a4b791e533316a5aac.

NASB Strong's Bible Text. La Habra: The Lockman Foundation, 1995.

Olive Tree Enhanced Strong's Dictionary. Spokane: Olive Tree Bible Software, 2011.

The British Cyclopaedia of the Arts, Science, History, Geography, Literature, Natural History, and Biography. Edited by Charles F. Partington. London: Wm. S. Orr and Company, 1838.

The Canadian Oxford Dictionary. Edited by Katherine Barber. Don Mills: Oxford University Press, 1998.

The Merriam-Webster Dictionary of Quotations. Springfield: Merriam-Webster Inc., 1992.

The New Bible Dictionary. Edited by D.R.W. Wood and I. Howard Marshall. 3rd ed. Downers Grove: Inter-Varsity Press, 1996.

Andersen, Karen. "Tea and Christianity." *Crisis Magazine*. Last modified 29 November 2012. http://www.crisismagazine.com/2012/tea-and-christianity.

Arnold, Johann Christoph. *Why Forgive?* Rifton: The Plough Publishing House, 2012.

Andreyev, Nikolay. "Ivan the Terrible." *Encyclopedia Britannica*. Last modified March 14, 2022. https://www.britannica.com/biography/Ivan-the-Terrible.

Augsburger, David W. *The New Freedom of Forgiveness*. 3rd ed. Chicago: Moody Publishers, 2000.

Austen, Jane. *Pride and Prejudice*. Public Domain.

Barna, George. *The Second Coming of the Church*. Nashville: Thomas Nelson, 1998.

Bernall, Misty. *She Said Yes*. North Farmington: Pocket Books, 1999.

Bolin, Brent L. "The Heart and Mind—What the Biblical Word 'Heart' Means." Faith Bible Ministries Blog. Last modified 6 July 2012. https://faithbibleministriesblog.com/2012/07/06/the-heart-and-the-mind-what-the-biblical-word-heart-means/.

Boyd, Greg. "One Church #1: Baptist to Anabaptist." *The Meeting House*. June 23, 2013. Podcast, video. http://media.themeetinghouse.ca/vpodcast/2013-06-23-870-video.m4v.

Bright, Bill. *Have You Made the Wonderful Discovery of the Spirit-Filled Life?* Peachtree City: Bright Media Foundation and Campus Crusade for Christ, 2008.

Brown, Adrienne. "How to mend a family feud." *Canadian Living*. Last modified 4 September 2012. https://www.canadianliving.com/life-and-relationships/family/article/how-to-mend-a-family-feud.

D.J.R. Bruckner, "The Stage: Hitler's Childhood," *The New York Times*. Last modified 25 September 1986. https://www.nytimes.com/1986/09/25/theater/the-stage-hitler-s-childhood.html.

Campbell, Roger. "The Unmerciful Servant." In *Preach for a Year #2*. Grand Rapids: Kregel Publications, 1993.

Carpenter, Eugene E., and Philip W. Comfort. *Holman Treasury of Key Bible Words: 200 Greek and 200 Hebrew Words Defined and Explained*. Nashville: The Livingstone Corp., 2000.

Chambers, Oswald. *My Utmost for His Highest*. Basingstoke: Oswald Chambers Publications Association, 1986.

Chernoff, Marc. "9 Things Happy Couples Never Think." Marc and the Angel Hack Life: Practical Tips for Productive Living. Accessed 19 May 2014. http://www.marcandangel.com/2014/05/18/9-things-happy-couples-never-think/.

Cloud, Henry and John Townsend. *Boundaries*. Grand Rapids: Zondervan, 1992.

Colijn, Brenda B. *Images of Salvation in the New Testament*. Downers Grove, IL: IVP Academic, 2010, as quoted by Cavey, Bruxy in "Life 2.0 #2: Wind and Water." *The Meeting House*. February 23, 2014. Podcast, video. http://www.themeetinghouse.com/teaching/archives/2014/life-2-0/.

Covey, Stephen M.R., and Rebecca R. Merrill. *The Speed of Trust: The One Thing That Changes Everything*. New York: Free Press, 2018.

de Saint-Exupéry, Antoine. *Le Petit Prince*. (The Little Prince) 1956.

Doidge, Norman. *The Brain That Changes Itself*. New York: Penguin Group, 2007.

Dostoyevsky, Fyodor. *The Brothers Karamazov*. Translated by Constance Garnett. New York: Lowell Press.

Drummond, Henry. *The Greatest Thing in All the World and Other Addresses*. Project Gutenberg, 2005.

Edwards, James R. *Pillar New Testament Commentary: The Gospel According to Luke*. Grand Rapids: Eerdmans, 2015.

Elliot, Elisabeth. *Through Gates of Splendor*. Carol Stream: Tyndale House Publishers, 1996.

Elmer, Duane. *Cross-Cultural Conflict*. Downers Grove: InterVarsity Press, 1993.

Endo, Shusaku. *Silence*. Marlboro: Taplinger Publishing Company, 1980.

Fee, Gordon D., and Douglas K. Stuart. *How to Read the Bible Book by Book: A Guided Tour*. Grand Rapids: Zondervan, 2014.

Fernando, Ajith. *Jesus Driven Ministry*. Wheaton: Crossway Books, 2002.

Frady, Marshall. *Martin Luther King Jr.: A Life*. New York: The Penguin Group, 2002.

Freud, Sigmund. *The Joke and Its Relation to the Unconscious*. Translated by Joyce Crick. London: Penguin Books, 2002.

Hicks, Robert. *Failure to Scream*. Nashville: Thomas Nelson Publishers, 1993.

Hingley, R. Francis. "Joseph Stalin." *Encyclopedia Britannica*. Last modified 14 November 2022. https://www.britannica.com/biography/Joseph-Stalin.

Holusha, John. "Students Killed by Gunman at Amish Schoolhouse." *The New York Times*. Last modified October 2, 2006. https://www.nytimes.com/2006/10/02/us/03amish-cnd.html.

Housel, Morgan. "6 Important Lessons from Nobel-Prize Winning Psychologist Daniel Kahneman." *Business Insider*. Last modified 11 October 2014. http://www.businessinsider.com/lessons-from-daniel-kahneman-2014-10.

Hughes, R. Kent. *The Sermon on the Mount: The Message of the Kingdom*. Wheaton: Crossway Books, 2001.

John, Tara. "JK Rowling Reveals Why Harry Potter Named His Son After Professor Snape." *Time*. Last modified 27

November 2015. http://time.com/4128152/harry-potter-son-professor-snape/.

Kershaw, Ian. *Hitler: A Biography* New York: W.W. Norton, 2008.

King, Martin Luther Jr. *Strength to Love*. Boston: Beacon Press, 1981.

Krauss Whitbourne, Dr. Susan. "5 Ways to Get Your Unwanted Emotions Under Control," *Psychology Today*. Last modified 7 February 2015. https://www.psychologytoday.com/intl/blog/fulfillment-any-age/201502/5-ways-get-your-unwanted-emotions-under-control.

Lewis, C.S. "Essay on Forgiveness." New York: Macmillan Publishing Company Inc., 1960.

Lieven, D., et. al. "Russia." *Encyclopedia Britannica*. Last modified 9 April 2022. https://www.britannica.com/place/Russia/Ivan-IV-the-Terrible.

Liggins, Stephen. "What We Can Learn from African Christians." *The Briefing*. Last modified 8 April 2013. http://matthiasmedia.com/briefing/2013/04/what-we-can-learn-from-african-christians/.

Limmer, Peter. "The Sign of Jonah." Sermon presented at Seaside Chapel English Worship Service, Itoman, Okinawa, November 2, 2014.

Loy, Aaron. "5 Really Bad Reasons to Leave Your Church." *Relevant*. Last modified 16 August 2016. http://www.relevantmagazine.com/god/church/5-really-bad-reasons-leave-your-church

Lucado, Max, as quoted on "Forgiveness Opens the Door for Change!" *Living More Abundantly.* Accessed 31 August 2019. https://livingmoreabundantly4christ.com/tag/forgiveness-is-unlocking-the-door-to-set-someone-free-and-realizing-you-were-the-prisonermax-lucado/.

Manning, Brennan. *Ruthless Trust: The Ragamuffin's Path to God.* San Francisco: HarperSanFrancisco, 2000.

McCann, Dr. Gillian, and Gitte Bechsgaard. "Don't Trust Your Feelings!" *Psychology Today.* Last modified 29 December 2017. https://www.psychologytoday.com/us/blog/return-stillness/201712/dont-trust-your-feelings.

McDowell, Josh. *More Than a Carpenter.* Wheaton: Tyndale House Publishers, Inc., 2009.

Moore, Beth. *When Godly People Do Ungodly Things.* Nashville: B&H Publishing Group, 2002.

Morgan, G. Campbell, as quoted in "Jesus: The Perfect Revelation at the Perfect Time?" Christiantiy.com. Last modified 30 September 2010. https://www.christianity.com/jesus/is-jesus-god/christophany-and-incarnation/jesus-the-perfect-revelation-at-the-perfect-time.html

Morris, Leon. *Pillar New Testament Commentary: The Gospel According to Matthew.* Edited by D.A. Carson. Grand Rapids: Eerdmans, 1992.

Muck, Terry C. *Sins of the Body: Ministry in a Sexual Society.* Vol. 19. Waco: Christianity Today, Inc., 1989.

Murphy, Francois. "Hitler's older brother was in fact younger and died early, historian says." Reuters. Last modified 31

May 2016. https://www.reuters.com/article/us-austria-hitler-idUSKCN0YL1WH.

Nauert, Rick. "Bitterness can make you sick." *PsychCentral*. Last modified 10 August 2011. https://psychcentral.com/news/2011/08/10/bitterness-can-make-you-sick/28503.html.

Nolan, Hamilton. "A Letter from Ray Jasper, Who Is About to be Executed." *Gawker*. Last modified 4 March 2014. http://gawker.com/a-letter-from-ray-jasper-who-is-about-to-be-executed-1536073598.

Payne, Leanne. *The Healing Presence*. Grand Rapids: Hamewith Books, 1995.

Payne, Robert and Nikita Romanoff. *Ivan the Terrible*. New York: Cooper Square Press, 2002.

Perry, B.P. "Why Was Ivan so Terrible?" *History*. Accessed 19 February 2022. https://www.history.co.uk/articles/why-was-ivan-so-terrible.

Peterson, Andrew. "Just as I Am." Released 25 February 2003. Track 5 on *Love & Thunder*. Essential Records, compact disc. Copyright © 2003 New Spring Publishing Inc. (ASCAP) (adm. at CapitolCMGPublishing.com) All rights reserved. Used by permission.

Peterson, Andrew. "The Chasing Song." Recorded March 2000. Track 2 on *Carried Along*. Brentwood Records, compact disc.

Preston, Gary D. *Character Forged from Conflict: Staying Connected to God During Controversy*. Edited by David L. Goetz. Minneapolis: Bethany House Publishers, 1999.

Ross, Kathy W., and Rosemary Stacy. "John Wesley and Savannah." Accessed 25 April 2016. http://www.sip.armstrong.edu/Methodism/wesley.html.

Sapp, Marvin, as quoted on "Marvin Sapp Quotes." AZ Quotes. Accessed 31 August 2019. https://www.azquotes.com/author/51012-Marvin_Sapp.

Schmidt, Alvin J. *How Christianity Changed the World*. Grand Rapids: Zondervan, 2004.

Seamands, David. *Healing for Damaged Emotions*, as quoted by Muck, Terry. *When to Take a Risk: A Guide to Pastoral Decision-Making*. Vol. 9. Waco: Christianity Today Inc., 1987.

Sebag Montefiore, Simon. *Young Stalin*. New York: Vintage Books, 2007.

Seltzer, Dr. Leon F. "Don't Let Your Anger 'Mature' Into Bitterness." *Psychology Today*. Last modified 14 January 2015. https://www.psychologytoday.com/blog/evolution-the-self/201501/don-t-let-your-anger-mature-bitterness.

Seltzer, Dr. Leon F. "Trust Your Feelings?…Maybe Not." *Psychology Today*. Last modified 8 August 2008. https://www.psychologytoday.com/gb/blog/evolution-the-self/200808/trust-your-feelings-maybe-not.

Smedes, Lewis B. *Forgive and Forget*. New York: Simon and Schuster, 1984.

Spurgeon, Charles Haddon. "Forgiveness Made Easy," *Metropolitan Tabernacle Pulpit*. Vol. 24. Pasadena: Pilgrim Publications, 1969.

Spurgeon, Charles Haddon. *Spurgeon on Prayer & Spiritual Warfare*. New Kensington: Whitaker House, 1998.

Stone, Daniel F. "The fiery partnership between two great psychologists can help explain why some relationships fall apart." *Quartz*. Last modified 27 January 2017. https://qz.com/896150/daniel-kahneman-and-amos-tversky-the-science-behind-the-fiery-partnership-between-two-great-psychologists/.

Stuart, Douglas. "Lecture 4: Out of Egypt and Into the Promise." Old Testament Survey I: Creation, Covenant, & Kings. Lecture at Ockenga Institute of Gordon-Conwell Theological Seminary. South Hamilton, 2005.

ten Boom, Corrie. *The Hiding Place*. Grand Rapids: Chosen Books, 2011.

Thielman, Frank. *The NIV Application Commentary: Philippians*. Grand Rapids: Zondervan, 1995.

Thomas, I.D.E. *The Golden Treasury of Puritan Quotations*. Chicago: Moody Press, 1975.

Wiersbe, Warren W. *The Bible Exposition Commentary*. Wheaton, Illinois: Victor Books, 1989.

Yancy, Philip. *Soul Survivor*. New York: Doubleday, 2001.

About the Author

VALERIE LIMMER LIVES IN OKINAWA, Japan, where she works as a missionary, sharing the good news of Jesus' love, hope, and salvation. Her first book, *On the Potter's Wheel*, was a memoir focusing on her first two years as a missionary in Japan.

Valerie is neither a therapist nor a theologian, but she has experienced severe abuse from a handful of people. In *Captive Set Free*, her second book, she shares many of the principles and techniques she's learned and applied to her own life on her journeys towards forgiveness.

In her spare time, Valerie enjoys writing, drawing, learning new languages, and making Japanese wax food models. She and her husband, Peter, are originally from the Greater Toronto Area, in Canada.

To learn more about Valerie's books, read her blog, or find out more about her missionary work, please visit valerielimmer.com.

www.ingramcontent.com/pod-product-compliance
Lightning Source LLC
Chambersburg PA
CBHW030033100526
44590CB00011B/188